PAPER

Some Marketing Advice

HEARTS

Beth Revis

A NOTE ABOUT WEBSITES

Throughout this book, the author occasionally refers to websites for further reading and resources. Please keep in mind that web content continually changes, and the author cannot control this.

For additional online resources, visit http://bethrevis.com/paperhearts

This book is dedicated to the writers
who want their words to
fill the silence.

Dei gratia.

Table of Contents

Introduction

After the Book Deal

Don't Lose Focus

Social Media

Book Release Marketing

Advertisements & Sales

Reviews & Events

In Conclusion

Introduction

Plot twist: A lot of "marketing" doesn't feel like marketing at all.

It's All About the Money

FOR SOME PEOPLE, bringing up money in the context of art is akin to cursing in church.

Look, I love my art. Writing is always first and foremost an art to me. I want to make beautiful art, and I want to share that art with the world. I care—deeply—about the cadence of language, the emotional pull of words, the significance of white space.

But I also care deeply about paying my mortgage.

And honestly? There's nothing wrong with that. Too many people gloss over the importance of actually making money in art. Sure, art is priceless, something that one experiences as a part of life. But art should also have a monetary value. The artist has worth. The time invested in the art has worth. The art itself has worth. And that worth needs to translate into money so the artist can continue to make art.

This book is about marketing. It will not make you tons of money, but it will, hopefully, help you get a few ideas that will help your book get exposure and therefore sales. There are a lot of books and seminars and workshops out there that are all about marketing on a larger scale. That isn't what this book is. This book is more of an introduction, covering the basics and giving you a launching pad to grow your ideas from there.

And while money may be a dirty word, it's a necessary one.

IT'S NOT ALL ABOUT THE MONEY

Although this book is about marketing—which will hopefully lead to sales—it's also worth noting that your *career* is not all about the money.

You are an artist. Your choices are made for art, not money. Your work has value far beyond the price tag. Don't get so wrapped up in cash that you forget about your art. **Marketing is nowhere near as important as writing.** If you have the choice between writing and marketing, write. If marketing is taking away from writing, quit marketing. Whatever you can do to market your work is nothing compared to the books you produce.

Art first.

Backlist Sells Frontlist

YOU'LL HEAR IT OVER AND OVER again—nothing sells backlist like frontlist. This means that the best way to move a book you've already published is to publish another book. With every release of a subsequent novel, I have seen sales uptick for past novels in print, regardless of whether they were self or traditionally published.

There are several reasons for this, but the main ones are quite simple. When you have a new release, you have something to talk about, and you're attracting new readers. Readers who were aware of your past books but hadn't gotten around to reading them are reminded of you, and start reading. Readers who weren't aware of your past book read your new one and look up other books you've written.

Any way you look at it, if you want to sell more books, write more books. Sales compound, and selling one book sells others.

All the marketing in the world doesn't make up for the very simple solution to just write more.

Is it Worthwhile?

YOU CAN EASILY SPEND MORE MONEY than you will ever earn on your book in marketing it. You can easily spend more time marketing a book than you would writing another one.

But is it *worth* it?

This book is an introduction into some of the basic things you can do to help your book gain an audience. But at the same time, I want to make very sure that you're not so focused on marketing that you forget about your art.

Because honestly? At the end of the day, there is a limit to how much marketing can help you. Think of it like a fine balance, where your time and money are weighed against how effective your efforts are. Don't invest too much marketing in a book at the expense of writing the next book or at the expense of frittering away your profits.

When their first book is released, many authors feel that they have to do as much as possible to help sell it. They bend over backwards, ticking all the boxes in an imaginary checklist, saying to themselves, *If I just do this, and that, and this other thing,* then *the book will be a success!*

But no. That's not how it works. The reality is that you can do everything, and the book still may not sell. You can do nothing; it may sell buckets. There is no checklist.

And the only one you're competing against is yourself.

The success of one book isn't comparable to the success of *your* book. You and another author are both selling books, but you're selling *different* books. You have different audiences. And at the end of the day, you're not competing against the other author. There is no competition. It's not like a reader will only purchase one book.

Marketing plans are highly individual—just as books are. Learn from what other authors do, emulate them, but know that you cannot measure your success—or lack thereof—against them.

Partner with Your Bookstore

NO ONE WANTS TO SELL your books more than you. You have the biggest investment in your career.

But you know what? Your local bookstore is also focused on selling books, and it only makes sense to work with them.

BEFORE YOUR BOOK COMES OUT

The best thing you can do to partner with your bookstore is *show up*. Go there to shop for books. Go to other author events and participate. Be a loyal customer. *This is the most important part of the equation; don't skip it.*

If your book is being traditionally published, consider going to your local indie with a copy of the ARC. Ask to speak to the book buyer in your genre. Introduce yourself, give them a copy of the ARC, mention who your publisher is, and discuss if you'd like to set up a book launch or other promotion through them. Don't be offended if they can't initially fit you in or are hesitant to do a promotion; bookstores have dozens of authors vying for their attention and schedules that book months out.

If you know your publisher's book representative in the area, consider reaching out to them as well; they may be able to facilitate a meeting or have additional ideas for promoting your book.

AFTER YOUR BOOK COMES OUT

Once your book is available, stay in touch with the bookstore. Work with the events planner to do a book launch or other events. Ask to be involved in the community, whether that be through school and library visits organized by the bookstore or helping in events such as Small Business Saturday (the Saturday after Black Friday, where small businesses often do a lot of promotion).

Also, work with the bookstore to provide signed copies of your books to readers who don't live in your area. If there's a special "signed edition" section of the store's website, ask if your books can be featured there. Include your bookstore's information and how to order signed books on your website. Make sure the store knows your contact information so they can contact you to sign additional stock or personalize books as needed.

And remember—just be involved. Your bookstore is part of your community, so treat it like that. Show up. Participate. Encourage other authors to do signings at your local bookstore. Encourage readers to visit the bookstore. You both have to same end goal—to sell books—so it only makes sense to work together.

BOOKSTORES & THE SELF PUBLISHED AUTHOR

If you're self published, I won't lie; it will be harder to work with a bookstore. Most self published authors get their income from independent bookstores' greatest competitor—Amazon—and there's some (justified) resentment there. If you only have ebooks for sale, it's unlikely that a bookstore, which profits from print copies, can form a good partnership with you. But if you do sell print copies, go to the store with a plan. Don't try to "trick" the bookstore into thinking your book isn't self published; they know. Instead, be up front about your book's origins, but also have a clear plan of what you can do with the bookstore in terms of promotion. If your book has local ties (such as being set in the area), that's a key selling point. If you have an established audience and can assure a crowd of a certain level to attend a signing, mention that. If you have a school-library program in place and want to reach out to the community, mention that. Come in organized and professional—most authors don't.

Know that most likely, your book will be sold by consignment. Rather than pay you for books from the start, they'll be on the shelf and you'll get a check once a book sells or on a set schedule based on sales. Be sure to ask about consignment policies at the store and make sure they're amenable to both parties.

On Exposure

THERE IS A DISTURBING TREND—particularly among online publications—to expect an author to provide literary work for free, paying them only in "exposure."

This trend can vary from blog tours to major online publications, but the end result is still the same: You give them words, they publish the words either online or in print and don't give you any money for them.

There are times when you *should* do work for exposure. When you're actively marketing a book, particularly near release time, you should also be actively looking for places to market your book. This is when blog tours, guest posts, and articles directly linking to your book come in. If the topic of the post is about you and your book, then there's a good chance you are actually benefitting from the exposure and shouldn't charge a fee. If you approach the publisher with the sole hopes of using their platform, then you're arranging a "for exposure" agreement.

However, if someone comes to you with a topic to write or something that will not directly and specifically market your book, money should be involved. If the only time you get to mention your book is in the by-line, you're not really getting exposure that's worthwhile. . . and even then, it's not that great. Your time will not be compensated with sales or even interest in your work.

Especially be wary of people who are building their *own* careers at *your* expense. If someone wants an article for an ad-riddled website, you can bet they're getting money from revenue that's not being passed on to the content providers—to you. If a "publisher" wants your story or poem in a literary magazine, they should pay you for it. Either they're making their money in advertisements or sales, or they're hoping to use your story to launch the magazine higher and then make money selling it. Regardless, *they* are profiting from *your* work, and you are getting nothing in return.

If you're trying to build a career, you could consider working for exposure, but consider the perception of value. When you provide work for free, the perception of its value lessens significantly. A career is rarely built on providing freebies; you need sales.

Money is often a topic that writers don't want to discuss. They're so grateful that people want to read their words that they are willing to give them away for the exposure. Money, some say, has no place in art.

If your hands feel dirty when they accept money for your work, just buy some soap with that money and wash them.

Have a Goal

NO MATTER WHAT YOU DECIDE to do to market your book—whether it be an advertisement or a contest or a social media campaign or anything else—go in with a clear goal of what you want to accomplish. It will dictate the best approaches you can take to achieve your goal.

GOAL: EXPOSURE

If you're struggling just to get your book noticed, then one approach to make people more aware of it is through social media. Create a graphic that showcases your book's cover and a small tagline or description. Encourage people to share the image by offering them a prize or other incentive.

Example: "Tweet this [message/graphic] by Friday afternoon and you could win a signed book!"

GOAL: SALES

If you're specifically after sales, you could consider doing a preorder campaign or a campaign where, after a certain amount of sales are reached, everyone gets a prize. This would work more effectively for a self published author who has direct access to her sales, but can be used in conjunction with traditional publishers. The prize could be something physical, or it could be a more universal reward, such as the release of an online short story.

Example: "With every copy of my book sold at this bookstore, you'll also get a signed bookmark!" *Or* "When my book hits a hundred sales, I'll release a free short story to all my followers!"

GOAL: FOLLOWERS

While I don't think it's smart to buy followers in social media, encouraging people to follow you can be helpful if done in a targeted way. Gaining more followers who actually care about your work (i.e. not random people who are being paid cash to follow you or doing silly follow-for-follow campaigns) can lead you to a wider audience. Don't overuse this method, but if, for example, you know you want to use social media to help promote a book that's coming out in a few months, it makes sense to boost your follower count as much as possible before then.

Example: "Sign up for my newsletter and get a coupon code for my latest book!"

GOAL: REVIEWS

Everyone wants reviews—they want more of them, and they want them to be good.

Resist the temptation to do too much specifically targeting reviews. If you hold a giveaway and the only way to enter is to give your book a five-star review, you're going to get yourself in trouble—you're soliciting for false reviews at that point.

You could offer a prize to anyone who reviews, regardless of star rating, but that also holds some pitfalls and some may interpret this as a subtle trick, assuming you'll only give the prize to someone who left a positive review.

While it's fine to want to thank reviewers for helping your work, approach any type of promotion that's focused on reviews with caution.

The One Percent

AT THE TIME OF THIS WRITING, I have 25,000 Twitter followers. None of them were bought—I have never paid for followers and *never* recommend that anyone do that. 25,000 different people individually clicked the little button to follow me on Twitter.

That number sounds like a lot. It gob smacked me when it scrolled up from 24,999 into that golden 25k. It felt like an accomplishment, one that I didn't deserve.

But you know what? It means nothing, really.

There's a perception that social media popularity results in sales. I see this across the board, from book publishers who get dollar signs in their eyes when they see a large following count to unpublished authors who believe if they can boost their following count higher, they'll earn a book deal.

But the truth of the matter? You're lucky if you earn 1% of your social media followers in sales.

When *The Body Electric* came out, I had roughly 30k followers across all my social media outlets, primarily Twitter, followed by Facebook and Tumblr, with Pinterest and Instagram trailing behind. I went all-in on a campaign to sell limited edition copies of *The Body Electric* with bonus content, including full-color commissioned illustrations. I used only my social media to advertise the campaign.

It resulted in 1% of sales. I had 30,000 combined followers across social media at the time, and I made 300 sales.

True, this was a limited edition that only had a print-run of 300, and there's the potential I could have sold more. But I think I pretty solidly hit my target market and served them efficiently, and I doubt I could have made many more sales beyond that initial 300.

I've seen this play out in other ways too. There are authors with a million followers on social media whose books don't hit the list. One percent of a million is nothing to sneeze at, but there's a big difference between a million and ten thousand. A million dollars will buy a mansion; ten grand will buy a nice used car.

This certainly isn't a hard and fast rule. And it is absolutely easier for authors with a larger social media following to build sales—I sold 300 limited edition copies of *The Body Electric*, but I would have sold none without that campaign, and those sales resulted in reviews and word-of-mouth sales that increased the book's success exponentially. I still have people who mention that campaign when they tell me they purchased the book a year later.

And there is also a point on social media where the 1% goes up—some authors gain such a strong following that they cultivate a group of people who actively buy their books whenever available. However, these blockbusters aren't selling books because they're good at social media; they have a lot of social media followers because they write good books that people want to read and have a strong personality that people want to listen to.

My point is: Numbers do nothing but inflate your ego. 25,000 followers are *not* 25,000 sales, and at the end of the day, your career is built upon *sales*, not *followers.* Don't break your back trying to boost follower numbers; they'll come when you continue to write books that people want to talk about and when you continue to post content that people want to read. It's not worth it to focus solely on building up more and more followers for just 1% of sales. Build a social media following because you want to join the conversation and be a part of the community, not because you want to sell to them.

ENTRIES DON'T EQUAL SALES

Just as social media numbers don't translate directly to sales, don't think that entries in giveaways and contests will translate either.

There are people who are "serial enterers." They see a freebie; they sign up for the freebie. They don't really pay attention to what they're signing up for, and even if they do, they have no intention of buying it.

Don't worry about them. You were never going to sell to them anyway. Don't let it hurt your feelings when you hold a Twitter contest and people unfollow you after the contest. Don't feel glum when you put a lot of effort into a Facebook campaign that goes nowhere. Don't concern yourself about the person who gets mad because you're offering an ebook and they want a print book. Just don't worry about it.

Control

THE ONLY THING YOU HAVE to do to have a successful book on the market is:

1. Write an amazing book
that a bunch of humans will love.

2. Have a bunch of humans aware
that the amazing book is out there.

That's really it. If you have the product people want, and people know you have it, then you can sell it.

The hard part is writing something that lots of people will like.

The hard part is also making them aware that the book exists.

For some people (arguably, to a degree, for *all* people), luck plays an integral role in discovery. Some people just flat-out get lucky, and their book is "discovered"—either by a handful of influential people who helped promote it (a major publisher willing to invest marketing dollars, a movie producer willing to develop it, a reviewer giving a big bump in sales), or by the masses who spread the book by word of mouth.

Aside from writing a brilliant book, you can't control who sees it. You can't control the way an audience will react; you can't control if it gets picked for promotion or movie development, or any of that.

But here's what you can control: touches.

TOUCHES

Just because you tell someone to buy your book, it doesn't mean they will. It'd be a lot easier if that's the way it worked . . . but it's not.

Instead, it will help if you consider a lot of your marketing efforts to be stepping stones that lead to a sale. I think in terms of five, and I picked up the "touch" marketing lingo over the year. Basically, someone needs to see or hear about your book five times before they buy it. This can be things you control—such as a tweet, a Facebook post, an event at a book festival you present at, a bookmark you mail to a bookstore, etc. It can be things you can't control, such as a publisher-bought advertisement or the holy grail of book sales—word of mouth.

Either way, you can't tell someone to buy your book. You can only provide them with a "touch" or a "step" leading to a book sale. You can post that tweet or go to that event. You build sales five steps at a time. Even if the person doesn't buy the book from you as you stand in front of them at the bookstore, they may buy it after they see it again on Facebook. You won't see them click the link on the post and purchase your book, but you had an effect.

Don't get disheartened when your marketing efforts don't lead directly to sales. They lead directly to steps, and you're putting the reader on the path toward your book.

TYPES OF TOUCHES YOU CAN CONTROL:

- Social media and online presence
- Events you coordinate and plan
- Your attitude and presentation at events
- Creation and distribution of swag and some marketing materials
- Advertisements and promo that you purchase

TYPES OF TOUCHES YOU CAN'T CONTROL

- Paid advertising from your publisher
- Your marketing budget/plan or lack thereof

- Where your publisher sends you on tour
- *If* your publisher sends you on tour
- The publisher's social media and online presence
- Blurbs from other authors
- Your book's bookstore presence (including whether or not your book is in a bookstore, but also end caps and displays)
- Your book's library presence
- Whether or not you get a film deal
- Whether or not you get a film made
- Whether or not you attend trade shows
- Whether or not you get foreign deals

TYPES OF TOUCHES NO ONE CONTROLS

- Word of mouth

It's this last one that's key. Nothing sells a book like word of mouth. Nothing. And you don't control that. Your publisher doesn't control that. It just…happens. You could do absolutely no marketing whatsoever and if you have good word of mouth, your book will sell.

But…you can't really affect word of mouth. You just can't. You can't *make* people talk about your book, read it, or recommend it to friends. You can't control whether or not someone will go into a bookstore, see your book, recognize it, and want it because someone they trust labelled it a "must read."

You have no power when it comes to the most effective marketing in the world.

But you can influence that marketing strategy. You can't engineer word of mouth, but you can provide a "touch." You can strengthen word of mouth by increasing exposure, by putting it on someone's radar, by creating a situation where someone will ask about the book, will be actively seeking it out, or will at least recognize it on the shelf when they pass by.

So when we talk about marketing books, we're not talking about the hard sell. This book is not a miracle that will guarantee thousands of purchases and fame and fortunes. All I'm really doing is trying to help you get another touch—

another way to reach a reader. Focus on the touches you can control that will lead to someone picking your book up and holding it in their hands.

Good marketing can't really make someone buy a book. Good marketing can just make someone pick it up and consider it. Only a good book can sell a book.

One Sale vs. Group Sales

THE STRATEGIES IN THIS BOOK are designed to be a jumping off point for authors regardless of their career path, but some strategies will work better for self published authors and some will work better for traditionally published authors. While one form of publishing isn't better than another, they are different, and targeting different marketing approaches often works to the author's advantage.

In self publishing, sales tend to be more along the lines of "one at a time." Interaction with individual readers on a one-on-one basis, small campaigns that are more personal, and being very in touch with the reader base works best for self publishers. The author is—at least in the beginning of her career—focused on moving ahead one sale at a time, hoping those sales compound into larger and larger sales over time.

In traditional publishing, sales tend to be more in bulk right from the start. The author needs to think in terms of moving not one book at a time, but hundreds or even thousands. Campaigns are more about reaching the masses, building a broad reach, and inspiring sales immediately rather than over time.

Because of these differences, marketing tends to be different for each mode of publishing.

But it doesn't have to be.

A traditionally published author should never ignore the one sale from an individual reader. The self published author may launch her career to the next level if she focuses on shifting her perspective to moving in bulk instead of small sales.

As you research the marketing that works best for you, try strategies that work for both modes of publication. While I have some elements divided out by chapters in this book, I encourage you to read it all. Learn from the strategies of authors who publish differently from you.

Don't limit yourself.

Marketing for Self Published Authors

NO SINGLE MARKETING PLAN will fit every book, but there are some strategies that tend to do better depending on your method of publication.

Self published authors usually develop their careers by focusing on multiplying sales over many books. When they release their first book, they will likely not make that many sales, but as they release each subsequent book, the series picks up steam and adds up. They will likely see their greatest spike in sales several months or even years after the release of their first book.

Because of that, one of the greatest marketing strategies for a self published author is to **release volumes of work in a strategic schedule.** Nothing boosts sales like releasing another book, so making sure that your work comes out quickly and regularly will help your readers become addicted to your writing. In *Paper Hearts, Volume 2: Some Publishing Advice*, I give a sample schedule of a self published author's release schedule, but I want to quickly reiterate here that you don't have to publish work as soon as you finish writing it; consider writing two or more volumes *before* you publish so that you know you can release them strategically over time.

Particularly when dealing with a series of books, it's vital for the self published author to work on **branding.** This means having a title for the series, having covers that work together, and having book descriptions that both clearly list which volume the work is, and what series it's a part of. An example of branding is the book that you're currently holding in your hands. When I worked with Hafsah at Icey Designs to develop the Paper Hearts series, I knew I wanted the titles to be very similar. We developed color schemes for the books, and Hafsah added a banner that indicated which volume number each book was. The result was a trilogy that no one could think didn't belong together.

When working with fiction, you'll likely have to be a little more nuanced with your book covers...but not that much. Take a look at the New Adult romance genre; they tend to have branding down to a science. Many New Adult romance covers look the same—a black and white photo that shows a close-up of an intimate couple with spots of color in the title and an ornate or eye-grabbing font. The entire *genre* is branded; a reader knows that a cover like that will be a specific genre with specific tropes. It's no different than when you go to a restaurant and see a little chili pepper beside the dish on the menu—it's a cue that the meal will be spicy. The black-and-white with ornate titles is a cue that the book will be spicy too.

So when you're coming up with your own book's cover, consider how you can translate that cover to subsequent books, and how that cover tends to align with the genre. It's all a part of your brand. Look at the popular books in your genre and compare their covers. You'll definitely see some classic tropes. YA will often have a girl in a pretty dress on the cover. Sci Fi tends to have a ship in space. Thrillers have huge titles that take up most of the book. Make sure you're looking at *current* titles, as trends change and you don't want your book to look dated.

Even if you're not writing a series, still brand your work. *You* are the brand. Make sure that your readers know what other books you have available in the **back matter** of your book—those pages at the end where you can list your previously published works. Add in sample chapters of other work—either past or forthcoming—as well as links to your website, social media, and newsletter.

Once you have your book's schedule and brand down, it's time to consider **pricing schemes.** There are a few simple tricks to use when you price your novel:

• **Set a price that can go on sale:** Don't immediately jump to giving away your book for free or cheap (i.e. $0.99) You're going to want to price a little higher for several reasons. First, there's the perception of value—if your book is cheap, people tend to think it's not as a good. Second, you want a price point that you can drop later on when you want the book to go on sale—this adds to the perception of value. If the reader knows the book was $4.99 in the past and it's being offered for $2.99 on sale, they're more likely to impulse buy the book.

• **Go cheaper or free for the first book:** Once you have multiple books out, consider changing the first book's price to free or cheap. Your first book is a loss leader; let it go to readers at a reduced rate so that they'll get hooked on the series and read the subsequent books. Remember, the key here is that you have multiple books in a series out *before* you create a loss leader. Your goal is to make up the lost profits with the sale of the subsequent books.

• **End all prices in 99¢:** This idea continues the perception of value. People are more willing to buy something that costs $4.99 than they are to buy something that costs $5.00. The one penny makes a difference; they perceive they are buying something that costs less than $5.00 (albeit by just one cent), and they are therefore more likely to buy it. So you should end all your prices in 99¢ as well. And that includes foreign prices. You will have the option to set foreign prices or have the retailer do it for you. I always let the retailer suggest the price (so that I don't have to do the math of conversion rates) and then I go through manually and change each price to the nearest 99¢ mark.

Once your book is published, with brand and pricing all set up in place, your next goal is **reviews.** Note that I didn't say sales—for a self published author starting out, reviews are more valuable than sales. This means you will likely need to give your book away for free to garner the reviews. Don't set your book's price to free; instead, approach reviewers and readers individually (or via your newsletter or social media group) and offer the book to them for free in exchange for an *honest* review. Note the emphasis on *honest.* Don't bribe people for five stars. Your book will do far better with honest reviews that run the gamut of stars than a bunch of fake five stars.

Don't worry too much if this step takes time—quite a bit of time, in fact. Reviews are notoriously difficult to come by, and you may have to have several branded books out before you'll get a significant number of them. Once you do have good reviews, it's time to look at **paid advertising**. At the time of this book's printing, hands-down the best (and one of the only) worthwhile paid review sites is BookBub.com. BookBub is a site designed for readers; it sends a daily email to readers who select which genres they like and shows them the top deals of sales for those books.

BookBub is quite expensive, but if you have a book that has multiple volumes out, is branded well, can easily go on sale due to its price point, and has good reviews, it can be a game changer. BookBub has a massive reach, and several successful self published authors use it exclusively to launch their careers.

Because it's so good, it's also difficult to get a BookBub advertisement. You have to apply, and most people are rejected a few times before they successfully nab a spot. Make sure you follow their submission rules to the letter.

There are other paid advertisers out there, and by the time this book is in your hands, there's every chance that things have shifted. Check out writing forums and discuss with other authors which sites work best for them. Some authors prefer to use a dozen or more smaller sites in place of the one big BookBub site, and if you follow that strategy, you need to really research which ones are legitimate and which ones are a waste of time or money. Remember that you often get what you pay for.

While doing an ad campaign, keep track of your money spent. Maintain this record with future ad campaigns and book releases. As a self published author, you should be seeing exponential growth with every ad campaign and subsequent book release. If you're not, reassess your material and your strategies.

Marketing for
Traditionally Published Authors

WHEREAS SELF PUBLISHED AUTHORS are looking to the future for their sales, traditionally published authors are looking at the here-and-now. Publishers are expecting sales right out of the gate, and most authors never see a larger spike in sales than during their debut week. Marketing plans are often, therefore, vastly different from a self published author; the goal is to garner as many sales as possible in the first few weeks—in fact, in the first few *days*—of the book's release. A large spike of sales in the beginning of the book's life could mean that the book has the potential to list in the *New York Times* or *USA Today*, but even if it doesn't it also signals to the publisher that the book has potential for more. It's not uncommon that an entire book's life is projected from the first week's sales . . . or from pre-order sales that happen before the book is even on the shelves.

I don't say this to terrify you—although I know it is terrifying. You're working for years on a book that has to prove it can win a race from the very first moment. But if your book doesn't have a huge opening week, that isn't an instant death knell. It may mean that the publisher will want to rebrand your book with a new cover. It may mean that the publisher will position the book differently, or shift the marketing plan to have a greater focus on a specific demographic, such as the school and library market. It's not the end of the book (or the world) if your first week's sales aren't there. But even so, that's where your marketing endeavors lie—in boosting those first week's sales.

First and foremost, **work with your publisher.** Let them know what you're doing to help your book. Do this for two key reasons: first, so they know that you are working and taking your job seriously. Second, so they can help. If you want to print bookmarks, approach them first. They may be able to provide you with designs or graphic help; they may be able to print them for you. If you have bigger ideas in mind, let them know. For *Across the Universe*, I wanted to do a big giveaway of books and asked for a larger number of ARCs. They sent me a case. If your publisher knows you're working to help the book's sales, it's in their best interest to help you do that. Keep them in the loop.

Building early buzz for your book is key. **Advanced Reader Copies (ARCs)** help you do that. ARCs are designed for reviewers to get a chance to read the book early on, write reviews, and help generate buzz. Your publisher should be handling most ARC distribution, but you'll probably get a handful of personal ARCs as well. Use them well—don't just give them all away to friends and family (even though they'll surely ask for a copy). Instead, come up with some ways that you can use your ARCs to help promote your book. This could be in the form of giveaways, contests, or simply going to your local library or bookstore and hand-delivering a copy.

You're also going to get people requesting ARCs, usually book bloggers. Unless you particularly want to, I recommend not giving them your personal ARCs, and instead collecting their information and passing it on to your publisher. Doing this will show your publisher how many people are interested in your book from the start, and it means they are footing the bill to send the reviewer the ARC. Of course, the publisher may not send the ARC—but with the buck passed, the fault isn't in your hands.

ARCs are valuable—they're more expensive to produce than hardcovers— so not every single person who asks for one can or even should get an ARC. When I have books that are out in the ARC stage, I tend to create an online form for people to request the ARC. I have them enter their name and address, so my publisher can easily mail them one, but I also have them enter their website or blog and relevant statistics, such as how many people visit the blog daily on average. I go through and highlight blogs that I think my publisher will most want to submit an ARC to. Ideally, it'd be great if every single person who requested an ARC got one, but realistically there is a limited number, and the purpose of an ARC is as an advertisement tool.

Also be selective of readers outside of the United States (or whichever country your publisher is based out of) requesting ARCs. I always feel bad about this, but it's very difficult for ARCs to make it past the American border. Remember that the ARCs are being printed by an American publisher who is marketing specifically to Americans; countries outside of America will have their own publishers, and you want those publishers to purchase your book and create ARCs for their country. Additionally, it's cost prohibitive—shipping charges can skyrocket very easily! I tend to have at least one international contest of an ARC—international readers can be very vocal about books they love online—but I do limit them.

After the book is published, you'll likely still receive requests for ARCs or free copies of your books. Be judicious at this point; a legitimate reviewer may require a book for publication review and any reviewer that you approach to request a review should be given a free copy, but other reviewers can purchase the book or check it out for free from their libraries.

In order to help push sales early on, **a preorder campaign** is common for traditionally published titles. Typically, a preorder campaign will offer readers who purchase the book in advance a small gift, such as a poster, a signed bookmark, or something else.

Most authors will either run the preorder campaign themselves or join with a handful of bookstores to run it. If the publisher decides to back the campaign, the publisher will likely organize it with specific bookstores. When a preorder campaign is run through a bookstore, readers get the free gift when they preorder from that specific bookstore. When an author runs it herself, she'll typically have people sign up to receive the free gift by mail after purchase.

If you run a preorder campaign yourself, should you require proof of purchase? In general, no. It's just not worth the hassle, and it will limit the number of people who enter. I tend to state on the entry form that, as the organizer, I can request proof of purchase at any time, but I don't require it up front and would only request proof if I suspect someone is taking advantage of the system (by request dozens of gifts for example). Make entering easy on both you and your reader; even if they didn't purchase the book, they're getting a targeted piece of marketing material that might encourage them to purchase in the future.

Also, make sure you're following the law. Some states have different rules about "gift with purchase" or "purchase required" giveaways, so make sure you're not violating anything with your campaign.

I have found that the key to preorder campaigns is to make the gift be something that's easily mailable and also exclusive to the preorder. It needs to be special, something to push someone over the edge in terms of purchasing. For *The Body Electric*, I paired with my local independent bookstore for a preorder campaign. The first three hundred copies of the book sold from that bookstore came with a special envelope full of exclusive swag readers couldn't get elsewhere—custom art cards made by three different artists depicting the characters of the book, a signed bookmark, a sticker, and a few other small goodies. All the swag fit in the package with the book (and since it came as a preorder, the bookstore just mailed the gift with the book, which meant I didn't have any additional mailing costs).

We sold out weeks before the book's launch date.

The exclusivity of the gift and the seamless integration with the bookstore made this preorder campaign a success. It was pricey, though—I essentially broke even, and the three hundred sales barely covered my costs in producing the gifts. But it also generated buzz, and people are still talking about the swag and campaign a year later.

Speaking of **swag**, this can be one of the key ways for a traditionally published author to market her book. There's a chapter later on dedicated to swag production, but very quickly, my top tips for swag are:

• Show at least a key image from the book cover, if not the entire book cover, on the swag. The title needs to be somewhere prominent as well—even on nontraditional pieces of swag, such as temporary tattoos.

• When possible, make it flat and sized to fit in a standard envelope.

• Include your publisher logo and the ISBN on bookmarks or postcards that are intended to go to professional resources (libraries and bookstores).

• Don't spend an arm and a leg on swag. It's a helpful tool, but if you're spending more than a dollar per piece of swag, you're losing money.

For a traditionally published YA book, **the school and library market** is a key part of your potential success. If you write MG, it's vital. Reaching this market can be tricky, and it's not that uncommon for a book to build its entire success around the school and library market, as opposed to bookstore sales. To hone in on this market, consider a **targeted campaign**. The common way to do this is by mailing postcards to schools and libraries.

This can add up quickly, though, and can be both cost prohibitive and time consuming. Consider honing in on schools and libraries in your immediate area, and rather than just send a postcard—which can easily end up trashed—send a note offering to do visits with the students or library patrons, offering to send bookmarks or materials for the classes to use, etc.

And speaking of **events**, they'll be a key source of income and promotion as your career progresses. Again, there's more information on events later on in this book, but I want to add here that one of the best things about the YA community is the tendency to do group events where a panel of several authors present rather than one author speaking to an audience. This style of event is ideal—less work, more audience attendance, and cross promotional opportunities across the genre.

Of course, if you can wrangle an invitation, **book festivals and conventions** remain a good way to gain exposure and sales. Your publisher may be willing to send you to some book fests, but don't be afraid to ask—let your publisher know you want to attend festivals (particularly if there's a specific one you have your eye on), and look up individual festivals and apply to go yourself, if your budget allows.

And while events can be helpful, they're not required. **Social media** remains a strong way for authors to reach a much wider audience than they ever could on their own.

The Changing Face of Marketing

Part 1: Be Wary of Advice

BE AWARE OF WHEN THE ADVICE you're given was first developed. A lot of people, for example, will quote agents who said "get a blog!" Getting and maintaining a blog *was* important . . . five years ago. Now, many agents actually recommend you quit wasting time on blogs. Blogs aren't read as often as they once were and have been replaced by social media and "micro-blogging." Additionally, blogs take a lot more work—work that could be better spent on the manuscript.

I still blog because I enjoy it, and because I still get something out of it. In fact, much of this book was written using ideas that I'd already blogged about. I think better when I write, and I find that blogging is a medium for which I can think and organize thoughts. But if I were *only* blogging in the hopes of book sales or exposure to agents, then I should quit.

At a convention, an agent mentioned how frustrating it can be to give advice and then to have people think that advice is *always* 100% right for *everyone* all the time forever. She gave an example of recommending authors get on Twitter. She had given this advice at a conference when Twitter was pretty new, and at the time, it was solid advice—new authors could get on Twitter, informally talk to authors and agents, build a network, etc. She'd emphasized Twitter because it was still new and some people hadn't heard about it before.

But since then, she's often had authors almost twist her words, taking them to mean that a new author *had* to be on Twitter no matter what. Even though the advice was several years old, the authors were taking it literally, emphatically believing that it was a requirement to be a successful writer. Some had included the information in their query letters to her, as if they were saying, "Look! I did what you said! Can I have a book deal now?" Others took rejections of their query as a sign that they needed to build up their Twitter following . . . not that their book wasn't good enough.

Marketing has changed—and just like everything else, now that we have the internet, it's changed *quickly*.

Another example of this: I still have notes from a convention I attended in my state SCBWI program, where the marketing advice person gave tips on Facebook and how to gain more readers. Facebook's own policies and shifting algorithms have changed so much that there was really nothing in her presentation that still applied to me when I was finally published a few years later. Her ideas for promoting a Facebook page were laughably out-of-date and in some cases in violation of Facebook's new policies simply because the program had changed that quickly.

On the flip side of this, I distinctly remember overhearing some published authors at a different convention laughing at Twitter and how it'll never take off, there was no point to it, and why would anyone waste their time on it? Those same authors are now on Twitter and loving it. I met one of them again after I was published and mentioned that conversation; she admitted that Twitter had far more power than she'd ever initially anticipated.

When I was first published, literally just a month or so after my book was out, I went on a retreat with a bunch of other authors. As a total newb, I asked for advice. "The one thing that never works," I was told, "is a newsletter. No one opens them, and they're all spam. Don't waste your time." But look at marketing advice for authors now, and newsletters top the list. They go directly to the inbox of the reader, and there's little chance a reader won't at least see it—as opposed to the rapid displacement of social media. Targeted newsletters to a few thousand is more effective than a shot in the darkness of social media to ten thousand.

As always, the best way to market an old book is by producing a new book. This is true of both traditional and self published works. There are ways to enhance exposure, but nothing trumps a good, new book.

And the biggest thing: **The advice in this book is not universal. Do what works best for you and your audience.** There are *always* exceptions to the rule. Some people are still able to turn blogs into book deals. Some people have been able to go from nobodies to *NY Times* bestsellers through the power of Facebook ads. Some people have done the exact opposite of everything I say and made a far bigger success than I have.

In fact, some people have proven the exact opposite of all this advice. Don't take it as a checklist of what to do and not do—take it instead as a jumping off point for you to find the path towards marketing that works for you and your book.

The Changing Face of Marketing

Part 2: Success Breeds Indifference

THROUGHOUT THIS BOOK, I list various different ideas on how to market a book. Some are general, and some are specific. Some will work, and some won't. You'll get an idea of what works best for you. I have relied mostly on Twitter in my social media, but I know other authors who have marketed more successfully on Pinterest. I enjoy doing live events with fellow authors; some are more comfortable doing them solo.

You'll be able to tell which approaches you are more suited for. But what may surprise you is that once you get a handle on marketing in your own terms . . . your marketing efforts may nosedive anyway.

The first huge giveaway I ever did involved several dozen books. I had tons of copies of my own book, plus lots of swag, with dozens of winners. I spent a couple hundred on shipping alone . . . and it totally paid off in sales. I got a lot of attention online for doing such a big contest all at once, and it built buzz that grew exponentially. I really do believe that giveaway helped put my book on the map during launch.

The next year, for the sequel, I did a similar giveaway. More books this time—I had two releases by that point, after all—and more prizes. It was coming out at the same time of year, and I cultivated entries the same way. I thought it would be a blockbuster; my readership had grown, after all.

The entries came dwindling in.

The first giveaway was a success because no one had seen anything like it before. It was new and exciting. In the year that followed, other authors did similar things. Even I emulated myself. And by the time I was ready to do it again . . . it was old news.

The next year, I switched it up, doing a "creative contest" that required fan art for entries. It was a new and shiny and different idea at the time—and the entries were awesome, something people still talk about today.

People grow bored and indifferent when something isn't new any more. When ebook readers first came out, they were a huge draw for prizes. An author who gave away an ebook reader could easily get hundreds or thousands of entries. Now . . . not so much. People have developed their own preferences for which brand of ebook reader they want to use, or they already have one, or they know they don't care to have one. It's not as big of a draw.

Same with platforms. When I first started out, Facebook was everyone's go-to platform. People were building fan pages left and right, there were whole books written on how to market to a Facebook audience. Then Twitter came along…and Tumblr, and Pinterest, and Instagram. And Facebook changed its policies and algorithms in a way that benefitted corporations with huge marketing budgets and hurt small pages run by individuals. People who spent years building up several thousand fans on Facebook could suddenly only reach a few hundred if they didn't want to pay to boost their posts.

Don't get comfortable with one type of contest, promotion, or advertising mode. Especially when it comes to large investments, try to approach giveaways and contests with new eyes. Your goal is to reach new readers; you can't do that by doing the same thing every time.

After the Book Deal

You've worked so hard to get to this point.
Don't panic.

When to Market Your Book

THERE ARE SEVERAL DIFFERENT opinions on when one should market a book, and there are a lot of different advantages and disadvantages to consider. In general, though, I recommend not heavily investing in marketing your book more than three months before its release.

TRADITIONAL PUBLISHING

It's *hard* to keep still about a book you've been working on for years; I know that first hand! But you should reach a few milestones before you heavily promote the book.

Until it's announced on trade publications or by the publisher, don't announce it (unless you have different advice from your agent or publisher). There are a few reasons for that—your publisher may be planning a larger announcement, and trade deal publications have a specific schedule to meet. Your publisher may want to wait to announce until closer to sale date, particularly if the publication schedule has bumped back its release. And, in the less positive category, there's also a chance your book will be cancelled. Even after you sign your contract, you're not guaranteed the book will come out— don't announce something that you may have to retract later.

For many readers, a book's not real until it has a cover, so there's not much point making noise about it until it's something they can visualize. Even then, though, resist the temptation to invest money in printing swag and designing promotion until you have a *final* cover. Covers change for a myriad of reasons, right up until the release date, so until you're certain that it's the final cover and has been approved through all the channels (including the book buyers), there's little point in investing in swag or print materials that may end up useless. A book cover is basically the brand or logo of the book; just like Coca-Cola wouldn't make an advertisement without their trademark logo, neither should you.

Until the book's three months before release, don't bother heavily promoting it—and really, save your best promotion in the month before and after release. There are certainly conflicting arguments on this, but coming from a reader's point of view, it's easy to get burnt out from seeing a book. *You're* excited, but you also know what the book is. But your reader doesn't. Readers are excited about new releases, but if you make your new book too in-their-face too soon before release, they quit caring. They can't read it yet—or worse, they assume it's already out and can't find it in the bookstore, so they forget about it. You only have so many times you can reach a reader before they start ignoring what you're talking about. Don't waste it on time before they can actually get their hands on the book.

SELF PUBLISHING

Don't advertise the book until you're 100% certain that it will be a book. Don't mention it until you know, without a doubt, that it will get written in a timely manner. You don't want your readers to get excited about a book that you end up not writing by a certain date . . . if at all.

In general, I think the better plan is to not mention the book at all until you have a rough draft done. Once the draft is done, you have a better idea of how long it will take for you to get the book on sale—at that point, perhaps just announce a season (such as, Coming Fall 2017).

Currently some, but not all, retailers offer pre-order options. Whether or not you use them is up to you, but until you have the book for sale (either as a pre-order or as a release), there's little point in spending time or money advertising it.

Blurbs

A BLURB IS WHEN ANOTHER AUTHOR endorses your book. Usually printed on the cover or first interior page of a book, a blurb lets the readers of one author know that they will likely enjoy your book as well.

To get a blurb, publishers and/or authors request them from authors. Some publishers will prefer to get blurbs themselves; some will ask the author to do it on their own. If you feel awkward contacting another author and requesting a blurb, don't worry. *Everyone* feels awkward. It's one of the most awkward parts of the whole business.

When you contact another author, first make sure they're okay with being contacted. Some authors state on their websites that they prefer all blurbs to go through their agent or publisher; respect that, even if the author is a friend. And even if the author is a friend of yours, make sure you approach them professionally. You are, after all, requesting help for your profession.

THINGS TO MAKE SURE YOU INCLUDE:

• **That you're requesting a blurb.** Don't beat around the bush. Be up front that you are offering the book to be read for a blurb. Include it in your email subject heading.

• **Deadlines.** It helps immensely for an author to know if she has two months or two weeks to blurb.

- **Available formats.** Is the book available in ARC form, or can you only provide an electronic version?

- **Why you are requesting this author to blurb.** You *absolutely* should have already read their book(s) to know that it's a comp title; explain why you think this author's readers would enjoy your book as well. Your reasoning for asking an author for a blurb shouldn't be "you're a mega-bestseller and I hope to cash in on it!"

- **The book's publisher or if the book is self published.** Some authors don't blurb self published books. Yes, I know it sucks. Move on to an author who does.

- **Who to contact with a blurb.** It can be you, if you're comfortable with that, but it's often more helpful for you to include your editor or publisher's direct email so that the author can send it to them. Discuss with your editor prior to this how they would like you to handle it. Even if your publisher asks you to reach out to the author for the initial contact, they will likely be the ones to send the ARC and handle the blurb.

- **Thanks.** Whether they agree to read or not, thank them for their time. As awkward as it is for you to ask for a blurb, for many authors it's just as awkward to agree to read—or to decline reading. If they read and the book's not their cup of tea, they have to decline to blurb . . . and no one likes giving rejection.

ETIQUETTE

If the author agrees to read the book: Send it as soon as you can in whatever her preferred format is and include a reminder of the deadline for the blurb. And then step back. Let her read. If you don't hear anything from her again, assume that no answer means no blurb. Maybe she ran out of time and didn't get a chance to finish reading. Maybe the book just wasn't her cup of tea. Maybe she forgot to read. Either way, this isn't the time for you to send reminders that she has to write a blurb by your deadline or to ask for updates on her reading.

If the author declines to blurb: Graciously accept. It's nothing personal. They may have even liked the book, but the timing was off; I know of several authors who can only blurb one to two books per season, and if your book was the third one they read . . .

If the author does blurb: Thank her! She's doing you a professional favor, and it's only polite to thank her for her time and work. You don't have to give her a gift or anything, but sincerely expressing your thanks is always appreciated. And since she's supporting your book, it would also be nice for you to support hers; consider doing some cross promotion.

Dress for Online Success

EVER HEARD THAT PHRASE, "dress for the job you want, not the one you have?" Well, the online world is like that too. Make your online presence fit the job you want, not the one you have.

The simplest form of this advice is simply: Be professional. But that doesn't mean you have to be devoid of personality or opinion. Check out some of the most popular users of social media in YA publishing—they have personality and opinions in *spades*. But they're also highly professional and present themselves in a professional way.

DON'T SET YOURSELF UP AS A "WANNABE" . . .

I get it—you're not published yet, and you want to be. But that doesn't mean you have to label yourself as a "wannabe." A wannabe writer (or a variation thereof) is one of the most common handles among aspiring artists. Before you link your online profiles to that phrase consider: do you want to always be known as a wannabe? In five or ten years, would you still want that title, or would you rather have the title that marks you as a success than a wannabe? Set your brand up *now* with your actual name, not a wannabe title.

. . . BUT DON'T BE DECEPTIVE

I remember a few years ago, an aspiring author developed an entire website around her book, complete with a professional book cover and a "coming soon to bookstores near you!" label. I—and many others—assumed this meant that she had picked up a publisher or had decided to self publish. When I extended congratulations, she told me that no, she was still looking for an agent, the cover was homemade, and the "coming soon" was just wishful thinking. When people started pointing out that at best, this tactic was confusing, and at worst it was deceptive, she shrugged it off—she wanted to give the appearance of being successful.

There's something to be said for presenting yourself in a confident, professional manner, but there's something else to be said about presenting a false front. You can present yourself as an aspiring author without tricking others into believing you have credentials you don't have. Simply be honest in the way you portray yourself and your career without aggrandizing yourself or demeaning yourself.

CONSIDER YOUR PROFESSIONAL SELF

Decide for yourself how you want to be perceived. If you're writing for children, you should consider whether or not you're willing to curse on social media. It's not a matter of "this is who I am, they can take it or leave it!" Think of who's following you online—not just children, but also teachers and librarians . . . people who may hire you to speak to their children, or may *not* hire you because they're worried you'll be inappropriate. You don't have to change the way you speak if you don't want to, but you should consider the possible consequences.

You don't have to monitor every word you ever write, obsessively worrying about what people will think of you. Because they truth of the matter is that people will think negative things about you no matter what you do. Just make sure you present yourself in a way that you feel comfortable with people building a perception of you. I joke often online using sarcasm, but I'm careful to not let it get mean. Unless it's something I'm extraordinarily passionate about, I keep my political opinions offline. When I do live events, I want my appearance to be fun—but still neat and professional.

It's not about censorship. It's about professionalism. I approach my online self the same way I approached my professional self when I was teaching. I don't post anything online that would have gotten me in trouble with the principal when I was a teacher. That policy has served me well.

In the end, *you* control your appearance, both in real life and online. Just actually *be* in control.

PRIVATE LIFE VS. PUBLIC LIFE

The issue of privacy also comes into play—and is something almost every author I know worries about. When it comes to how much of your life you're willing to show online, the decision is yours and yours alone. Some people prefer to keep a closed door on their home life, some people want to be more open. It's up to you.

Keeping it Private: It's honestly difficult to keep your life private in this day and age, but not impossible. Get comfortable with privacy settings on social media. Use lists, and keep your data and pictures not only restricted in who can see them, but impossible for others to share to a wider audience. Get very comfortable with privacy settings, and when in doubt, don't share.

Opening to the Public: Even if you decide you're open to people seeing more of your private life on social media, I still think it's a wise idea to separate your professional and private life. Remember that your readers follow you online because they like your books, and while your kids are cute, having all your social media be nothing more than family life may feel weird to some people, almost as if you're putting them in a position of voyeurism. If you're using social media publicly as an author, people will expect a level of professionalism from you that they don't expect from the average person.

Remember that it's easier to start from a private platform and open up to a more public platform. Your privacy settings are like glitter—once you open the container and throw it out into the air, it's almost impossible to get it all back into the jar.

Website Basics

IT IS MY PERSONAL BELIEF THAT at the very least, an author should have a static website. This website should include the most basic information, and should exist primarily as a reliable source of information controlled by you.

Publishers may develop websites for you or your book—mine made a brilliant website for *Across the Universe* (see http://acrosstheuniversebook.com). But you won't be in control of it. It'll likely not be updated after that book, especially if you leave that publisher.

Instead, it's very important for an author to have a website she controls. It needs to be a place to compile *all* her books, regardless of publisher. It need to be a place where she can feature the kind of information that she wants. And it needs to be branded to her, not to just one book. (You can see mine at http://bethrevis.com)

There are two things to consider when developing your website. **First:** professional doesn't equal fancy. It's easy to drop thousands on a website design, but is it worth it? Typically, you'll find that new authors will invest a lot of money for a custom design, but as an author's career goes on, she's far more likely to simplify. A clean design that presents information professionally doesn't require a lot of custom code and art—in fact, often it just clutters the message you're trying to present. Don't invest money in a design over having good, quality content.

Second: carefully decide if you have the skills to do it yourself, or if you have to hire out the design and/or maintenance of the website. The preferred option is to have a website you can control—if you can't do it all yourself, hire a designer who can provide you with a format that you can edit. Typically, this means the website developer will give you a frame—their design is inside of a WordPress, Blogger, Wix, or similar theme that enables you to easily edit the content on your own. If you have to pay someone else to 100% do the work of your website, including editing small details, you're likely going to be losing more money than your page could ever earn you. This option is, however, attractive to people who have zero capabilities of doing any website content and are unwilling to learn.

In developing your website, consider the following pages and features:

• **A domain name that is as close to your professional name as possible**. Don't make the domain name be your book title—books are a one-time thing; *you* are a career. Try to make it be your name—mine is bethrevis.com—simply because that will often be the first domain people will look for. If you publish by your initials, use your initials (jkrowling.com). The name should match what's on the cover of the book. If your name is already taken, consider adding "books" or "author" to the domain name, or something else that will be easy to remember. Also, consider looking into whatever social media platforms you have, and attempt to make your user name be the same as your domain name across the board.

• **End in .com.** Even if you have to compromise on the domain. People will remember YourNameBooks.com sooner than they'll remember YourName.net.

• **Spend the extra money and time to make your own domain.** Don't be bethrevis.wordpress.com when you can be bethrevis.com.

• If you know the very basics of making things online, **use a site that you control and edit.** WordPress is a popular choice, as is Blogger and Wix. You want to be able to make additions or corrections and updates to the website whenever you want. If you have zero capabilities or comfort in doing this, you can hire someone else to update your website, but be aware that's added cost and time.

• **Make it look professional**. Suzanne Collins is often cited as proof that you don't need to have a snazzy website, and that's true. But you probably didn't write the next *Hunger Games*. You *can* have a bare bones website and be fine, but most templates are free or cheap and easy to use. Consider your website the basis of your online self—make it look good.

• **Make sure the most important features are very visible**. For many authors, this will be the cover of your latest book and a link to sign up for a newsletter. Whatever's most important to you requires the most prominent position on the site.

• **Don't spend too much money.** This is a mistake I've made more than once. The first website I made cost me literally thousands of dollars for an artist to make custom art and build a completely unique site. And it looked *good*. But not that much better than the website I built myself for less than a hundred a few years down the road, when the custom site no longer matched the type of books I was writing. You don't need to blow a lot of money to make a website that works. If you have it and want to, fine, but it's not necessary.

There are various bells and whistles that you can add to a website, but the bare minimum would be:

• **Contact page.** Whatever form of contact you're comfortable with. Typically, this will include either an email or a form for people to fill out. If you have an agent or someone handling rights, their information goes here, too. If you have a marketing contact who will handle ARCs, add it here. I also include my social media links and one-sheets in this area of my website, as well as my standard rules on how to hire me for presentations or visits.

• *Should you use a "contact me" form, or your email address?* Personally, I dislike contact forms and think they cut down on potential opportunities. In the past, I've organized some group giveaways. I wanted to email all the authors I was friendly with on Twitter that I wanted to invite to the giveaway in one big, group (bcc) email. Three or four of them had only "contact me" forms, which meant I had more work to do to reach them—especially the ones that also had captchas. One of the forms even required not a regular captcha, but a separate "alternate captcha" that required me to actually download a new plugin—just to contact the author! It may sound harsh, but it was far simpler for me to get a few different authors than to jump through the hoops to contact these.

- *If you can handle it, consider getting a "fan mail only" email address.* I have two emails: one for business and personal use, and one for fans. The one for fans is the one you can find online. This cuts down on spam in my professional address, enables me to send a custom vacation message to fans if I know I won't be able to keep up with correspondence (such as during a tight deadline), and keeps me organized.

- *Should you have a mailing address?* Don't put your home address online. That's just not safe at all. But many authors use post office boxes to accept fan mail, and that is a far safer alternative. You could also talk to your agent or publisher about accepting fan mail for you.

• **Bibliography or books page.** You want a complete bibliography of published works. There are various ways to do this, so check out other author websites for tips. I'm a fan of having a landing page for all books, then people can click to see more about a series, then click to read more about each book individually. I also include space for published short stories in anthologies or online.

- *If you're not published yet, a few sentences about the book and its status (work in progress, querying) is fine*—but don't give too much away, don't give it a fake cover or the appearance of having already been published, and don't have too many titles up there. You don't want to show a potential agent that you have dozens of trunked novels—you want the attention on the one or two titles you're actively working on.

- If you are published, I *highly* recommend you *never* talk about a book until it's got a pre-order button on major sites and a way for people to buy it. First, it's a waste of time, but second, things change. Even if you have a contract, that contract can be cancelled. If it's a work in progress, it may not sell. Don't put yourself in an embarrassing situation. There's no point in talking about a book that people can't buy yet.

• **About or bio page.** This does not and should not be your life story. But keep in mind that when you're published, people are going to want to have a few sentences to copy from your bio and add at the end of interviews or include on information for signings, etc. Your bio page absolutely should have a super-short biography that's no more than five lines long. Put it up top and make sure it's easy to find.

• Also include at least *one professional-looking headshot, along with photo credits.* This doesn't have to be an expensive photo-shoot, and it certainly doesn't have to be the stuffy-author-with-leather-patches-on-a-tweed-jacket type of photo. But it should be a clear face shot that shows who you are and is a high enough resolution to include in printed materials.

You're welcome to include other features on this page, such as a longer biography, a list of fun facts about you, or a FAQ. But just remember that people who are trying to feature you in media need that short bio, so make it easy to find.

And finally: make sure your website is up-to-date. You don't need to have constant updates here, but your events page does require maintenance, and your book page should absolutely tell readers about your latest and upcoming scheduled books. If your website shows the book you published two years ago and doesn't even mention the title coming out next week, you have a problem.

A Planned Website Map

WHILE THOSE THREE PAGES—contact, bibliography, and bio—are the bare minimum you need to showcase your work and make it easy for people to buy your books and find out more about you, most people are going to want to put more on the website. Here's one map that has worked well for me, but remember that you're looking for something that works best for *you*. Websites are very fluid and can fit any need!

When planning your own website, consider making a map of everything you want to feature. It will make it much easier for you to ultimately develop your website, whether you do it yourself or hire someone else.

LIST OF PAGES

- Landing Page
- Books
- Events
- Bio
- For Writers, Readers, and Educators
- Contact
- Blog

LANDING PAGE

This is the first page people see when they go to my website. The point of this page is to be clear, simple, and welcoming.

• *Graphic*: The page is predominantly taken up with a graphic that features my name and is used across all my social media and branding. The site itself is very simple, mostly black and white with a few blue accent colors, so this graphic is the way for me to "brand" my website.

• In a footer, I have three columns that feature:

- Tweet stream, a simple widget made by Twitter that shows my tweets and includes a "follow" button.

- A subscription link to my newsletter and a link for people to see a sample newsletter.

- An "Ask Beth Anything" box powered by Tumblr that allows anyone to ask a question that's then sent directly to my Tumblr.

BOOKS

Every author has some form of "books" or "bibliography" page, and nearly all of them are organized differently. Someone with one book will have a very different books page as someone with a dozen different series in different genres.

• *Buy links*: the goal is book sales, right? Don't hide the buy links. Make sure to make your indie bookstore link prominent—and if you can, work with a local indie store to provide readers with a chance to buy signed copies. Include all other major retailers, and don't forget Book Depository, a site that provides free shipping internationally for your foreign readers.

• Somewhere on your website, also include information on how people looking to purchase foreign language or subsidiary rights can contact your agent.

• Your main Books Page may show one book, or link to several. How you format that is entirely up to you. If you have series listed on your book page, and then have a separate page for each book, make sure that each book's individual page stands on its own. If someone directly links straight to that page, make sure it's possible for them to have all the information they need, including buy links, even if it's a touch repetitive. Some additional information that should be included with each book includes:

- Book cover: If possible, link it to a hi-res version of the cover.

- Synopsis of book: Consider copying exactly what's on the back of your book.

- Publisher name

- ISBN number

• Additionally, an individual book page could include:

- Blurbs

- Awards and accolades

- Links to sample chapters

- Imbedded trailers or other promotional materials

Keep the page as informative but clutter-free as possible. Remember that primarily, people are looking for: the book cover, the synopsis, how to buy the book. Keep that in mind, and make that information most prominent.

EVENTS

If you're doing live or online events that you want people to participate in, you have to make sure they know about them. Keep this area neat and organized, making sure to provide links with more information if needed, specific times and locations, and anything else someone may need to attend. Bonus points if you can directly link to a single event, so when you spread the word, you can send people specifically to that one event's information.

ABOUT / BIOGRAPHY

At the very least, you need to have a short blurb bio that people can pull to add at the end of interviews and in promotional material. This can be the same bio used in your book.

A headshot with photographer credits that people can use for print and/or online media should be included.

Some other fun things that you might want to add:

• Fun facts about you—the blurb bio has to be succinct, but you can still show your personality on this site

  • A longer bio, if relevant and you want to share

  • FAQ about you or your book

  • Links to social media

FOR WRITERS

Although entirely optional, many writers enjoy sharing either their story of publication or advice to other writers. Some suggestions for this section may include:

  • Links you've found particularly helpful in your journey to publication

  • Quotes or art that inspires you

  • Articles about writing and publishing you've written, or links to other people's works on the topic

  • Links or information to writing organizations to which you belong and which you recommend to others

FOR READERS

Again, optional, and likely something that you'll develop as your publishing credentials grow. Some possible suggestions include:

  • Insider details about the books, such as hidden "Easter eggs" and details for readers to find

  • A list of things that inspired you, or an article about where you got the idea for your novel

  • A gallery of fan art

  • FAQ about the book

  • Fun activities linked to the book (more common with MG or picture books)

FOR EDUCATORS

Consider adding this section especially if you write YA or MG and want to target the school and library market. Include information on:

  • Teacher's guides

- Lesson plans

- Classroom visit information

CONTACT

I've spoken a bit already about what should go on a contact page, but here's what's on mine. This is arguably the most important page on the whole website, so think carefully about the organization of it.

- Contact information, specifically an email address. I also include a PO box address

- Social media links

Typically, people are reaching out to contact you for a reason. Try to anticipate the reason and provide the information alongside the contact info:

- Rights availability

- Information on how to request an appearance

- Information on how to obtain a signed book

- Downloadable information:

  - Hi-res image files of all book covers

  - Hi-res image files for headshot, with photography credit

  - Press kit for books, if available

  - One-sheet for books, if available

SIDEBAR

On every page except the homepage, I have a sidebar that features the information that I most want to make accessible to my readers:

- Subscription link to my newsletter

- My top four social media links

- A list of places where my books are available to buy

Head Shots

EVEN THE CAMERA-SHY should consider getting some professional headshots done. You'll use them for several different purposes. If you're traditionally published, your publisher will likely want headshots to include in marketing materials (not that you have to be a model, but it may be good to pair your headshot with your biography or in "meet the author!" materials). And keep in mind—if you're going to be traditionally published, get your headshots done ASAP; your publisher may need them before you even finish editing the book, and it's better to be prepared than to have to scramble at the last minute (trust me on this, I speak from experience). If you're self published, you have the option of including your headshot in the back of your book or not, but either way, for both types of publications, it's a good idea to have some headshots of yourself available on your website. Not only does it help illustrate your "about me," page, but when people do online interviews with you, they're going to want to have a picture to pair it with; bookstores will want to add your photo to their events advertising; curious fans will seek it out; you'll likely want to use your own photo for avatars for online social media profiles; and so on.

For these reasons and more, make sure that you have a high-resolution file of your photo, and make sure that you have it easily available to readers on your website for download.

COSTS

You don't have to use a professional photographer, but of course you're welcome to, and many authors opt for that route. Costs will vary depending on your location, but remember that most author photos these days are not the stodgy old formal portrait in front of a background. If you have a friend with a high-quality camera, ask her to come over and snap some shots outdoors or in front of your bookcase—it may be just the right thing, and it's worth trying before you line up a pricey photographer.

CREDITS & RIGHTS

Whether you pay several hundreds for your headshot or you get your best pal to snap some photos one casual afternoon, you need to have two things to use the photo for your professional purposes: the rights and proper credit. Make sure you get—in writing, even if this photo came from your bestie—that you have the rights to use this photo for print and online media (and if you're doing this on a contract, clarify what your photographer means by noncommercial and commercial use, just to make sure there's no issues in the future). Also check with the photographer's preferred way to get credit, and make sure that whenever you use the photo, you include the credit to the photographer.

STYLE

There are several different styles of headshots, and it's up to you which you prefer. You may want to check out the websites and back covers of authors in your genre—but make sure that they're *recent* books, not books from ten or thirty years ago. Styles have changed a lot!

Formal: This was most popular several decades ago. The headshot is usually the bust up, with the subject sitting in a posed, formal way, and a typical photographer background behind her. The author is usually also dressed very professionally, such as in a suit, with conservative make-up and hair. A lot of people immediately think of this style of headshot when they think "author photos," but you should really question if it's appropriate for modern audiences. Headshot trends have changed a lot, and this style tends to make an author look stuffy and unapproachable.

Posed informal: This style is most used by authors today. The photo is still not a casual snapshot—it's obvious the picture was taken with careful lighting and by a professional—but it's not stuffy. Many authors will opt to have this photo taken outside, in a fun, dynamic place (some of the most amazing photos I've seen of authors were done at a shoot on a construction yard!), but posing in front of your bookshelf or with a stack of books is still popular. And the pose tends to be far more casual—this is about looking friendly and approachable. Smiles or even shots of you mid-laugh can be charming; staring off into the distance with a dour, contemplative look may not look as appropriate for this style. Many people will opt for more casual clothing but still have professional make-up and hair, keeping in mind that photographs tend to wash out the skin, so a little more definition of eyes and lips is usually much better.

Casual: This style of photo is far rarer—or at least, far more rarely used to effect. There are some great casual headshots out there, but be discriminate. Make sure the photo actually portrays you the way you want to be presented, and remember that even if you use a casual snapshot, you still need to give the photographer credit and have permission to use the photo. Also, be aware that when it comes to print material, you will need a high resolution file of your headshot.

DIMENSIONS

It's best if you can get a few different takes that can be used, but in general shoot to have at the very least a portrait and a landscape photograph that would work for print and online media. Different magazines or online articles will want the different dimensions based on their formatting, so if you can easily provide both, that's a great option to offer.

Also consider trying to have one photograph that works well if trimmed to a square size—this size is often used in flyers and brochures for events.

In terms of resolution, images should be saved at least 300 pixels per inch (often abbreviated as 300 dpi).

Graphic Design

BOTH ONLINE AND PRINT MEDIA works better with good graphic design. Books may be all text, but to sell books, you need images.

If you can, it will really behoove you to learn basic graphic design skills—and fortunately, there are a lot of resources out there with which to learn. For graphic design, the most popular programs are Adobe products (particularly Photoshop) or Gimp (which has the added advantage of being free).

For even simpler design functions, there are online programs that have pre-made templates you can easily use. Canva.com or the Word Swag apps are great resources.

If learning graphic design isn't your thing—which is fine, it is a skillset that takes time—select the pieces of graphic design that are most important to you, and pay a designer to make them for you. This is often the first thing authors do when designing print materials, but they forget about online marketing as well, and that's a mistake.

I'm not going to list any dimensions here because they change frequently, particularly for social media. A simple Google search will give you the most up-to-date dimensions to use for your specific social media needs.

In addition to designing swag, you can use design to make the following:

A MULTI-USE HEADER

I wanted something that showed my name and my book covers to put on various different places that readers may see it. I currently use this design as a

Twitter header, a Facebook header, and the header for my newsletter sign up and for each newsletter. When I noticed that Tumblr mobile uses a different design from the template that you select and can have a unique header, I uploaded this graphic there, too.

These platforms all have slightly different size requirements, but the image I used had enough white space to make it stretch to fit across them all. It's also boxier and not thin and narrow, making it work well for social media headers, and making all my social media branded to my name and book covers. All I had to do was upload my book covers to a white background and add my name.

ANOTHER MULTI-USE HEADER

I hired a graphic designer to make a header for my website—it was simple, but I wanted something that looked really clean and professional. This is the header that fronts my welcome page on my website, but I also used it at the top of my blog, and I turned it horizontal to be a part of my Twitter background. When Wattpad changed the dimensions of its header images, it was easy for me to upload this graphic at the top bar.

Additionally, this style and size lent itself well to print media—while I like having a bookmark for each individual book, I also wanted one bookmark that contained my entire bibliography, so I put this header on the front, and a small image of each book cover on the back, and bam, an easy bookmark, ready to print.

SQUARE GRAPHICS

If you teach yourself only one type of graphic to make, master the square graphic. Square graphics are the most universal; Instagram uses them, and they display nicely on other social media platforms.

One of the the things I did for the launch of *The Body Electric* was hire my graphic designer to make a basic square template featuring the book cover elements, and then I added in lots of different quotes, highlighting key words with an alternative color. Uploading it to Instagram and then feeding it into social media made for an easy, graphic advertisement during release month and became a key part of my marketing strategy.

Square images also tend to be the right size for most avatars.

BANNER GRAPHICS

I use these the least often, but they definitely help promote your work. Small rectangle-sized images work well in Twitter and Facebook particularly and can stand out in the deluge of square images—a square image tends to get cut off, but a correctly-sized banner ad will display the entire ad in the reader's newsfeed. Banner ads also lend themselves well for a line of text and the entire book cover.

In addition to just using these graphics in regular social media:

• Most social media (particularly Twitter, Facebook pages, and some Tumblr themes) allow you to "pin" a post to the top of your profile, so that someone clicking on you for the first time will see that post first. Something with a graphic element is a great post to pin.

• Whenever you do a giveaway, do a graphic as well—make sure it shows your book prominently, even if you're also giving away a lot of other books. Also make sure it includes a text link to your website where people can go for more information—you never know where the graphic may end up shared.

• Always take a look at your online graphics and see if they'd work well for print, too. In addition to using my website header as a bookmark, Penguin once made a Facebook banner for the Across the Universe fan page—which fit perfectly on top of a postcard and showed the different books amazingly. Square graphics in particularly could make great stickers.

Remember that print graphics do need to have a higher resolution than online graphics, and you should get permission to use something online in print materials if you didn't make it yourself.

Don't Lose Focus

Not everything after your book deal is about
marketing to earn a buck.

Step Back

WHEN YOUR FIRST BOOK COMES OUT, most people are only concerned about one thing.

Sales.

"How's the book doing?" your mom asks.

"How much money are you making?" that random Facebook friend asks nosily.

"When can we buy a boat and live a life of luxury?" your husband asks, just before you punch him in the throat because he should know better.

Of course sales and profits are a very key part of being a career author. You cannot continue your career without the financial support sales creates.

But at the same time, you shouldn't have a career if the only thing you care about is money. You have to care about the words before you care about the numbers. If the bottom line is the bottom line for you, you have a job, not a career.

Your Worth has Nothing to do with a Price Tag

THERE ISN'T A PRICE TAG that will adequately cover what your book costs.

You invest your *self* into your art. Your life. Your experiences. Your feelings.

You invest your time. You spend far, far, far more time writing a book than a reader will ever spend reading it. You agonize over words that readers skip. You carefully debate the use of a comma that most readers are oblivious about.

You invest your heart. Your words mean something to you. They are important. And you create them with passion and soul and heart, and there will be a reader who dismisses them entirely and calls them stupid and gives you only one star and a negative review and then forgets about the book entirely.

There is not a monetary amount in the world that equals what your book is to you.

. . . But there is also not a price tag that will cover what it means for a reader.

A reader who cries over the pages, smearing the ink. A reader who clutches the book to their chest, thankful to finally have proof that they are not alone in the world. A reader who stays up at night, their aching, tired eyes dancing over the letters, promising to read just one more chapter . . . just one more . . . just one more . . .

What we do isn't about the money. We will never be paid the money that is equal to our work, because there is no money equal to art. But at the same time, we will never be able to understand just how valuable our words are to our readers. Mathematics, dollar signs, and equations don't apply.

Find Your People

ONE OF THE BIGGEST GOALS you should have when starting your career has nothing to do with money. It's about people. Build a community. Surround yourself with readers and writers who are inclusive. Network not as an opportunity to get more money, but to build friendships.

ONLINE

Social media remains one of the easiest ways to find your people. Search hashtags based on writing or based on books or genres that you love. Join chats and participate in programs. The more you just show up, the more involved you are, the more you become a part of the writing community.

Don't be afraid to tweet or post to other authors. Some may not respond, but some will. Approach online communities like big social gatherings. Don't be a wallflower, too afraid to join in the conversation.

At the same time, don't be a shouter. Would you want to approach someone at a party if all they ever do is talk about themselves? No. An online community is about a *conversation*, not an elaborate ploy to spam people into buying your product.

Not everything has to be about your book—and, frankly, not everything has to be about books at all. People want to talk to other people who are passionate about *things*, so talk about the things you care about. Talk about your fandoms, your hobbies, the things you do, the places you go. Your conversations don't have to revolve around your book. If you wrote a book about Henry VIII, sure, talk about the time you travelled to England and saw the Tower of London, but also talk about that really delicious curry you had down the street, and what it was like watching *Doctor Who* on British television instead of Netflix, and how weird the Tube smells.

In short: Be interesting. No one wants to hear about you, you, you, but they want to hear about your experiences and thoughts and opinions. No one wants to be sold your book, but if you're a part of a community, people do want to support their communities. Participate in a real, authentic way and add something to the conversations around you beyond just "buy my book."

IN REAL LIFE

It's important to find your people in real life, too.

Go to your local bookstore and library and join the community there. Show up. Go to signings. Purchase books. Become a regular. When you go to the signings of local authors, introduce yourself. Ask to meet up for coffee, or just exchange social media info. Support the people around you who love books, and they'll support you too.

Go to book festivals and conventions—even if you're not presenting. There's nothing stopping you from being in the audience. Don't try to steal the show—this isn't a sneaky way for you to get some marketing in. You're a reader, too, right? So go to book festivals and conventions as a reader. Participate in the community you want to be a part of. If you make connections that lead to an invitation in the future, great, but go with the purpose of participating, not taking over.

Join organizations that are focused on writing. You still have a lot to learn, and you have ways to give back. Consider joining groups such as the Society of Book Writers and Illustrators (SCBWI) or other writing communities and participate in them. Don't forget that some groups will be seasonal—many areas have writing groups that pop up around National Novel Writing Month (NaNoWriMo).

Participate in writing retreats. Writing retreats are an excellent way to meet other writers and form lifelong friendships.

Just ask. I know. It feels like all *these* writers are cool kids. They sit together at lunch and wear pink on Wednesdays and there's no room for you. Except that's not how it is at all. 99% of the time, the writers I've met are kind, gracious, and gregarious. If you want to participate in something, just ask. Be professional and friendly, and you'll go far.

Online Community Groups

THERE ARE SEVERAL DIFFERENT ways to join online communities. Don't feel that you have to spend all your time online—remember, the most important thing you can do is write the next book—but when you're looking for a way to participate, these are some places where you may find your people.

SOCIAL MEDIA

Twitter chats. People use hashtags (#) to keep up with chats. Twitter automatically creates a link out of a hashtag, and clicking on the hashtag will take you to a page that displays all the conversations involved with that hashtag. Any post you make that includes the hashtag will then be seen by other people who are following it. Sometimes hashtags are used casually, such as the #amwriting hashtag, where people just post in correlation with updates on their projects. Some hashtags are more focused, timed events, such as a weekly chat for people who like a certain genre. And some hashtags are spur-of-the-moment spontaneous events. Keep an eye on what people are talking about, and jump into the conversation when you're ready.

Facebook groups. There are two types of Facebook groups—those that are open and those that are private. You can search for open groups and request membership. Closed or private groups require an invitation. Be respectful of group privacy. Note that you have to be a part of groups with your profile and real name, not a fan page or pseudonym.

Tumblr fandoms. If you're in a fandom, Tumblr is where your people are. Search the tags for things you like, especially media-based, such as movies, TV, and books. Tumblr is designed for sharing, so reblog the things you love and use hashtags to help people find you.

Pinterest boards. Pinterest isn't just for the classy crafters. Many authors post inspiration boards, writing tips, and book recommendations. If Pinterest is your thing, find other authors and jump in.

As with most online communities, you'll discover that the best thing you can do is just show up and participate. Don't be shy! You have nothing to lose!

REDDIT

Reddit is a huge network of forums, and it can certainly seem daunting. Keep in mind that each individual forum, known as a subreddit or simply a sub, is its own entity, moderated by its own group. Some subs are bigger than others, but look for the types of conversations more than the size of the sub. The YA Writers subreddit is well moderated and a vibrant community that welcomes both established and new authors; you can join at http://reddit.com/r/YAWriters

LIST-SERVS

If you join a professional organization, such as SCBWI, chances are they have an email list-serv already established. List-servs will go straight to your inbox, but are a wonderful way to reach other writers directly. You may want to consider asking other writing friends which organizations have the best list-serv; it's sometimes worthwhile to join a group just for an active list-serv.

FORUMS

There are several writing forums out there. The most well known are the Blueboards[1], KBoards Writers' Cafe[2], and Absolute Write[3]. Each has its own

---

[1] Full link: http://www.scbwi.org/boards/index.php

[2] Full link: http://www.kboards.com/index.php/board,60.0.html

[3] Full link: http://absolutewrite.com/forums/activity.php

personality and caters to different types of writers; check them out and determine if you'd like to participate in any of their conversations.

CREATE YOUR OWN

The Internet is a big, big place. There's nothing stopping you from developing your own writing community. Find a platform, recruit fellow writers, and just start. Most of the best stuff online comes from people who did just that.

Writing Retreats

FOR ONE-ON-ONE INTERACTION with authors, writing retreats are fantastic. They typically last about a week, and include a group of writers hanging out in a vacation rental house. Some lean more heavily on the work side, as people spend all day writing and revising; some are a little more wine-influenced, but either way, writing retreats are fun!

And don't be afraid of organizing your own retreat. If you'd like to spend some time on a writing retreat, contact some writing friends, pick a location, and *go*.

CASUAL RETREAT

A casual writing retreat is loosely organized. There may be some scheduled writing time, or the people attending may naturally fall into a rhythm of writing during certain times and relaxing during others. These retreats are excellent ways to recharge and re-inspire; surrounding yourself with other writers writing helps you focus, and the conversations you have after writing time are invaluable.

FOCUSED RETREAT

Some retreats are designed with a purpose, such as critiquing and revising or developing pitches or by genre. These retreats will likely have a schedule of events and everyone is expected to participate; I consider these retreats to be more like an intensive work time, as I focus in on one specific aspect of writing. If a casual retreat is like going to the gym in order to walk the track with your friends, a focused retreat is like going in with the intent to pump iron.

WORKSHOP RETREATS

Workshop retreats are a combination of retreat and conference. They include writing and social time, but also organized workshops, usually by published authors or other publishing professionals. Workshop retreats provide one-on-one learning time in a focused environment and are usually designed to help authors take their careers to the next level.

FOR MORE INFORMATION:

Go to WordsmithWorkshops.net or MadcapRetreats.com

THINGS TO PACK FOR A WRITING RETREAT

Writing retreats tend to happen in vacation rental houses, so they usually have all the amenities you need to get by. But they're not hotels that have been designed with travelers in mind, so make sure you bring an extension cord or power strip; there are never enough plugs. You may also want to bring a lap desk if you know you need a hard surface as tabletop and desk space may be limited.

Keep in mind that you're going to be with other people, people you're usually not around as you write. I always travel with noise-canceling headphones. As fascinating as the other people on the retreat may be, there will be times you want to focus, so bring whatever it takes for you to focus on your writing.

And don't forget the corkscrew—those wine bottles won't open themselves!

Network for Education

NETWORKING IS NOT ABOUT SALES.

It's about *education*.

The value in your connection with another person in your profession is *not* in what they can do for you. If you approach every opportunity you have to meet people or participate in events in this way, you're a tool. It's not about what others can do for you; it's about what you can learn.

A great example of this is debut groups. When I sold my first novel, I was invited to participate in an online debut group. There are several new ones each year for debut authors to participate in. I eagerly joined my debut group, which consisted primarily of a group blog and regularly scheduled private chats.

My first thought was: How can this help me sell books? I thought the group blog may have enough of a following to gain traction. I jumped in to help and participate, all the while keeping at least one eye open for sales opportunities. As my book's launch grew closer and closer, I tried to see ways I could leverage this network into sales . . .

And then I realized what an idiot I was being.

The value of my debut group did not lie in sales. In fact, aside from other members of the group supporting me, I don't think I got any sales at all from my participation. Instead, the value in the group lay in the knowledge we shared and exchanged. The public group blog did very little, but the private chats, where we were all honest and open, became a crash course in publishing and writing. I learned so much from just listening to others as they shared their experiences.

Currently, I'm a part of a private Facebook group of authors. There are weekly posts where members put up their book covers and discuss which books launched that day, but those tend to be about celebrating with the author, not purchases. People don't participate in the group in order to get sales—it is, after all, a private group that no one but us can see. Instead, we're there to learn from each other. We network so that when we have a question, we know who to go for answers. We share what we learn, what worked and didn't, what we hope the future holds.

This is the real value of networking and community. It has nothing to do with marketing and sales, but the knowledge you gain can help you be a better marketer and make more sales.

Don't approach every opportunity you have as an author as a chance to sell a book. Instead, consider what knowledge you can gain. Learning *how* to better sell your work is more valuable than trying to turn everything you do into a sales pitch.

Social Media

The quickest and most accessible form of online marketing available to authors today.

Don't Get Obsessed

WHEN IT COMES TO SOCIAL MEDIA, there's one simple rule: **You don't have to do anything.** This is my soapbox, and I find myself getting on it more and more lately. I do social media because I like it. I don't do it to "win" readers or "gather followers" or any crap like that.

The analogy I use is this: social media is like a cocktail party. Come to the party if you want to. At the party, meet new people, reconnect with others. It's a business party, so it's okay to talk shop, but it's not okay to monopolize the conversation and push yourself or your product on other people. Be polite. You can be a social butterfly or a wallflower; you can come with a thousand friends or not. It's up to you. You don't want to come to the party? Don't. You want to leave early? Do.

So my point is: **you don't have to do anything.** *You don't have to do anything.* But if you *want* to learn more about social media, then here's a little bit I've picked up on the way.

As writers, success is nebulous and relative. We cling to any indication that what we're doing is working, that we're reaching readers, making a difference, and surviving in this incredibly tough career.

Unfortunately, the data that's easiest for us to have access to—numbers and statistics—isn't really that relevant to our success.

Don't get obsessed by numbers.

These are the quickest numbers to access and the easiest to compare to other people. *Don't do that.* There will *always* be people who have more followers and subscribers than you do *and it doesn't matter.*

Those numbers are often out of your control. Someone randomly tweets you, and bam, you have a hundred more followers. You state a simple opinion, and bam, you've lost followers. You send out a post and get a dozen unsubscribes. Who cares? People have a lot of different reasons for following you, they have a lot of different reasons for *not* following you, and you'll kill yourself trying to figure it all out.

And it's pointless to compare followers. You don't know how people got their followers. Maybe they paid for them. Maybe they are witty and entertaining and people love them. Maybe they do the follow-for-follow bullshit that does nothing but plump up follower counts. Maybe they got featured somewhere and said something smart and gathered a lot of positive traction. *You don't know*, and it doesn't matter, because you're not them.

RANKS

It's also super easy to look up and compare your rank with other authors. For example, on Amazon you can look up your author rank, your bestseller rank (your rank compared to every other book on Amazon), your rank within categories, etc.

It's also super easy to drive yourself crazy this way.

REVIEWS

Most authors will advise you to never look at reviews, and there's a reason for that. Not only do negative reviews depress many authors, but they also lead to comparisons—*that* author has more reviews than me, *this* author has more five stars.

I talk more about reviews later in this book, but remember: you can't force anyone to read your book, much less like it. Reviews are for readers, not writers, and obsessing over them is a waste of time.

SALES

Indie authors in particular have access to sales data, particularly real-time, daily-updated data on sales. Which is nice, but also crazy-making. If anyone knew the perfect sales formula, they'd be making millions and laughing at us newbs. But as it stands, no one really knows exactly how to sell books, not even the most successful publishers. We know word of mouth sells, we know high concept sells, we know generally the kinds of things that create sales, but we all also know that a book can have everything going for it and still not sell, that crappy books that have nothing going for it sell like hotcakes. No one really understands. So try your best, but then move on.

WHEN TO CARE ABOUT NUMBERS

If you're running a giveaway or promotion, you should keep track of your numbers in a relevant way. If your giveaway is targeted on gaining more social media or newsletter subscribers, absolutely keep track of them during the time frame of the giveaway. If you're running a sale on your book, obviously keep track of what you're doing and how it affects your sales and ranks.

You do need to know if the work you're putting into promotion is actually helping. You need to know if the time and money you invested into it was beneficial.

But if you're so obsessed that you're checking it every day, getting bummed out or depressed over your numbers, *step away*.

And one final bit of advice that works across social media platforms:

Be aware of what feeds where. Look, I get that there are a lot of venues for social media. But—you don't have to do it all. You don't have to be everywhere. So if it's overwhelming, don't do it. Or just do part of it.

But what you shouldn't do is do one thing and feed it everywhere. *Example*: you only blog. You feed all your blog posts through Twitter, Facebook, and Tumblr. You never post anything on Twitter, Facebook, or Tumblr—you only use it to feed your blog.

Don't expect much from social media if you only use it as feeds for your blog. People can just follow your blog and ignore the rest. I have new, different content on Twitter, Tumblr, and my blog. Go to any of my social networking sites, you get something different. Some people subscribe to all four. Some just subscribe to one. That's cool. When I've got something big going on—a book launch, a big contest, etc.—then I cross-post to everything. My audience for the occasional rare big thing is exponentially larger then.

The Hard Sale Doesn't Work

WHEN WAS THE LAST TIME you bought something because a person you barely knew told you to buy it?

We're in the age of spam; people today are *very* adept at not only ignoring the hard sale, but also of actively removing it from their lives.

If all you ever tweet is "buy my book!" I'll unfollow you.

If all you ever post about is you and your book, I'll unsubscribe.

The hard sale—constantly just talking about your book and spreading sales links—doesn't work. No one wants to listen to someone who's just trying to prey on their wallet.

So what works?

Authentic engagement. Being an actual person instead of being a salesman. If I like you as a person, and generally like the things you're saying or the stuff you're doing, I don't mind it if you tell me every once in a while that oh, by the way, you also have this book for sale. In fact, your engagement has probably made me *want* to support you and your work.

The best approach isn't to think of social media and interaction with readers as a potential billboard for your book, but instead as a way to be social, participate, and have fun—occasionally mentioning your book. People are more likely to buy your book if they like your personality rather than if they are told to buy it from someone they barely know, whose only goal is clearly to sell them something.

Passion. Maybe you're passionate about selling your book, but I hope you're *more* passionate about your writing, your characters, your story. People respond to passion. Show your passion in an authentic, true way, and people will listen to what you say. By this, I mean, don't say, "I love my book! Buy it!" Instead, talk personally about why you wrote it, what it was like, what inspired it, or more generally about writing and publishing and the process of creation. That's the kind of passion that people are attracted to.

And, the greatest sales tool of all—**a great book.**

How do YOU Buy Books?

THE OTHER DAY I DID something shocking and strange.

I bought a book.

"That's not shocking and strange!" you might exclaim.

Well, true. It's not. Especially for me. But here's the kicker: I bought a book written by an author I had never heard of. This author had NO blog, NO Twitter, NO Facebook. NOTHING.

Are you shocked yet?

Probably not.

How many times have you gone into a bookstore or logged onto Amazon and just picked up a book not for the author's name, but because the book looked interesting? Most people buy books that way.

I bring this up because many people ask variations of the same question: how many followers do I need to have before I become a bestseller?

The answer to that question is simple: *none*.

A blog, or Twitter, or Facebook are not a book. Readers want a book. A *good* book.

"But!" some of you say, "But! They might want me more if I have a book and an online presence!"

Maybe. I can honestly say that I've bought some books only because I knew the author through her online presence first. And we all know of stories where someone was "discovered" because of her blog (or whatever). But chances are, that's not the reason why you'll be found. Sorry. But statistically, *many* more writers are "discovered" because their book is good, not because of their online platform. (And wouldn't you rather be known as the writer with the amazing book, rather than the writer with the blog?)

Think about yourself when you go into a bookstore. Don't you usually buy a book because the book looks good, not because you know the author online?

Yes, online social media can help. But you should do it because you like it, and you should do it in such a way that writing always comes first. You never have to apologize for not being a good blogger, or for not even having a blog. In the end, never forget: the book sells the book. Not the online media.

So Why is Social Media so Prominent?

IF NUMBERS DON'T MATTER, why is social media so touted by publishing insiders, from indie pros to agents and publishers?

IT'S EASY

Social media is an easy marketing plan, for both self and traditional publishers. It's easy to integrate, it's easy to implement. Much like blog tours, social media has become a standard form of advertising in the book world—whether or not its effective. It's *something* to do, it's not hard to do, so why not try it? Some people have found great success in social media promotions, and anyone who's innovative enough to stand out in the crowd can continue to find success. It doesn't guarantee sales—no method of advertising does—but it's not difficult, costs nothing, and likely won't hurt sales, so why not try?

IT GIVES A SENSE OF PERSONALITY

I was at a conference recently, and someone asked the agent giving the presentation why having a social media presence is such a common piece of advice for aspiring authors who are seeking representation. Her reply was first that the advice came from several years ago, when people weren't sure how effective social media could (or couldn't) be, but that she still likes seeing social media just as a way to get an idea of the author's personality and to see if the author has an idea of how to use social media. It wasn't so much about not signing an author until she has a certain number of followers; it was more about making sure the author knew how to use social media for when she *does* get more followers after publication.

By this, I'm also not talking about how many pictures of puppies you post—I'm talking about ensuring that you're not crazy, racist, or likely to fly off the handle and become a liability. The only time your social media will hurt you is if you show that you're not the kind of person who should even be on social media—it has nothing to do with how many followers you have, but with what kind of person you are.

IT CAN HELP—IT'S ONE MORE TOUCH

I talk about the touch theory of marketing several times throughout this book, but basically, it's the idea that someone has to see or hear about your book a certain number of times before they'll buy it. Social media is one more touch. Your tweet about your book's inspiration won't sell the book by itself, but it'll be a building block towards that sale.

Tagging Isn't Personal

ALMOST ALL SOCIAL MEDIA provides the ability to "tag" a person. If I make a post and tag you in it, you see the post, whether you follow me or not.

When you're published, you end up being tagged a lot by people you don't know. People who've read your book.

People who hate your book.

It can feel like an attack. You're just scanning your Twitter or Facebook and suddenly you see that someone's sent you a link to a review of your book. You click on it, and you read all about everything they hated about every aspect of your book. Or maybe they just tag you in a conversation they're having with someone else, about how they want that other person to never bother reading your book. Or how they hate your cover. Or how they bet your mother is a hamster and your father smells of elderberries.

And all of that adds up and adds up and feels like an attack.

It's not.

Because you, personally, were tagged, it can feel like the person is trying to get a response out of you, trying to rile you up, or trying to cast you in a bad light. Typically, though, they're not. Just because you're tagged doesn't mean they wanted or even realized you would see the post. Many people assume that authors don't run their own social media or get so many messages they won't see theirs. Some readers don't even think about authors as people at all.

People legitimately forget that authors are people. They *do*. When they write up a review—even a hate-filled negative review—and they tag the author in the review, they're often doing it for the sake of being complete. They're thinking in terms of categories, not humans. It's the same as providing a link to where you can buy the book or including a picture of the book cover in their review. They're not trying to hurt you-the-person, they're just trying to include the author's information in their post, forgetting that the author is a human who will then see the post.

So ignore these types of posts. If you don't like reading reviews, don't. You don't have to respond.

This bears repeating: *You don't have to respond.* Just because you get tagged in a post doesn't mean you have to respond to it. If the response it elicits is one of anger or sadness or anything less than positive, *you can ignore it.* You probably *should* ignore it. You don't have to interact. Chances are, the post-writer never expected an interaction in the first place. And even if they did, ignoring it is the most effective way of making it go away.

WHEN IT IS PERSONAL

There are a few cases when ignoring the hate won't work. It is rare, but sometimes people do take a negative review too far, turning their opinion into online bullying.

If you can, consider the age of the post-writer. YA authors have a large teen readership, and teens can be very passionate. If someone starts being inappropriately rude and hateful online, and you can tell the person is a teenager, it's worthwhile to attempt to correct the person. Saying something like, "you may not be aware of it, but I can see your posts and they are very hurtful" may be just the gentle reminder the reader needs to see that you're human.

But if it doesn't stop, if the person is intentionally trying to hurt you, you need to take further steps. Block the person and report them to whatever level is appropriate—whether it be merely reporting to the social media platform or reporting to the police. Just because you're an author, and therefore something of a public figure, doesn't mean you have to be exposed to hate and certainly doesn't mean you should allow yourself to be online bullied. Discuss with your agent, publisher, and other writer friends for further help. Screenshot everything. If the online bullying progresses to something more dangerous, such as stalking or obsession, seek professional aid and the police.

Like I said, it's rare that this happens—but it can happen. First and foremost, be safe.

Branding

MANY AUTHORS SPREAD THEMSELVES out over social media. A website, a blog, Twitter, Facebook, Tumblr, and more. Whenever possible, brand yourself across platforms so people can easily identify you.

Brand with your name, not your book's title. Book titles change—even after publication, in some rare cases. But more than that, your career is in your name, not one book. Don't tie up all your social media accounts to one book—as exciting as this one book is, you will move on.

Try to have the same user name, and try to make it just be your name. If you're "Beth Revis" on your book cover, try to be "@bethrevis" on Twitter and "@bethrevis" on Tumblr and other social media platforms as well. This isn't always possible, but if you can, do it. It may be wise to base this on your URL—whatever you use as the domain name for your website may work well as the handle for your social media.

Use a graphic to tie your social media together. For many people, the simple solution is to use your book cover for your avatar across all social media platforms. This is effective, certainly, in both branding and advertising your book, but if you'd rather use an image of yourself, try to use the same image across all social media.

Caveats

SOCIAL MEDIA CHANGES *FAST.* The following information was applicable at the time of publication, but could be out of date tomorrow.

Seriously.

In the following examples, I give opinions about which medias have worked best for me, some strategies, etc. But that all changes and evolves. When I started getting into writing, blogging was king. Now, I don't recommend that people blog unless they really want to. Currently, Twitter's doing amazing things; before that it was Facebook. Who knows what's going to happen next?

And even if the trends point one way, that doesn't mean they're universal. I was on Facebook recently, complaining about Facebook (as one does), and another author said Facebook was her greatest resource and has great success from it, not experiencing any of the problems I'd faced. Facebook's effectiveness changed for *me*, but not *her.*

Find what works for you and use that.

Don't rely on one platform. Any one platform can become ineffective over time. For me, as I just mentioned, that was Facebook. Facebook's policies have shifted, making it difficult for people who fan your page to actually see your posts unless you boost them—in other words, unless you pay Facebook to show your post to your own fans. Some people built their entire social media and marketing platform on Facebook, but when Facebook changed its policies, they found it harder and harder to reach the very fans who *wanted* to hear from them.

Does this mean you should spread yourself thin over every social media platform there is? Absolutely not. Instead, make sure to control the things you can control—your own website, your own newsletter. And don't treat any social media as a total support to your marketing plan; at best, it's a crutch.

You don't have to use social media. You will likely, at least at one point in your publishing career, be told that you "should" or "have to" use social media. Some authors get pressure from their agents or publisher; some authors get pressure from advice or marketing plans that "require" social media.

Social media is a tool, and it can *sometimes* be effective.

But it is not at all worth your writing career. Or your sanity.

Unless your contract stipulates social media use, keep in mind that, aside from writing the book you're contracted to write, you have no obligations, including social media. If your publisher pressures you to use social media and you're not comfortable doing it, talk to your agent. If your agent pressures you to use social media and you're not comfortable doing it, remind her that your relationship is a business partnership and you're not her employee. If someone says a marketing plan relies on social media, remember that no marketing plan is foolproof.

Don't replace your writing career with social media. The thing that makes you money, the thing that is your career, is your novels. Not your Twitter or your Tumblr or your Facebook.

It's the books.

The books are the art. The career. The important thing.

Don't lose sight of that.

A VARIETY OF SOCIAL MEDIA

In the following chapters, I talk about the social media I use the most often. But there are a lot of other options out there. Some others include:

• BookLikes: a page similar to GoodReads

• GooglePlus: Google's response to Facebook. There's a growing community here, and the use of Google Hangouts could be really inventive for readers and authors to integrate.

• LinkedIn: I really don't know why or how people use LinkedIn for writing, but some do, I guess?

• The Next New Thing: There are a lot of platforms out there, and things are always changing. Even if you don't anticipate using a new platform, sometimes it's worth logging on and grabbing your user name, just in case the next new thing becomes the next big thing.

Twitter

TWITTER IS THE MOST MIRCO of micro blogging. You basically have 140-characters to make a brief statement. Remember the cocktail party analogy? Twitter is the best example of that. You drop in, you drop out, you talk with other people.

Link: http://twitter.com

SETTING UP YOUR PROFILE

There are three key things to add to your profile where you can show your book and your personality: the header image, the avatar image, and your bio. Your bio also has to be short, like a tweet, so keep that in mind. Make sure to include a link to your work. Your header image is a great place to feature images of your book or a tagline. Your avatar could be a square image of your book cover, your headshot, or anything else. Try to make your twitter handle be your name with no spaces—that's the most common handle, and what many people will assume is you.

THE BASICS

• When composing a tweet, it will go out to all your followers in their newsfeed. Unless you start your tweet with an "@" symbol, which you would do if you were replying to someone.

• To reply to someone, have the @-symbol followed immediately by that person's twitter handle. It does *not* have to be in the beginning of the tweet—if it's anywhere in the tweet, the person you're replying to will see it (unless they block you).

• If you make a reply to someone that you want all your followers to see, put anything in front of the @-symbol. Example:

- "@bethrevis: Hi!" Will only show up in the newsfeeds of anyone who follows both you and I. It's still public, but harder for most of your followers to see.

- ".@bethrevis: Hi!" Will show up in the newsfeed of anyone who follows you.

• If you and someone else is mutually following you, you can send that person a Direct Message (DM). Only you and that person can see the DM, and it's the only non-public way to speak to someone on Twitter.

• Hashtags (#) can be relevant (i.e. #kidlitchat) or they can be funny (i.e. #youseewhatididthere) But remember: less is more. A hashtag will create an automatic link in your tweet, and clicking on that link will take you to everyone else who's used this hashtag recently. It's great for if you're following a chat or participating in a meme or joining a conversation about a hot topic. It's also great to use it to just be funny. But don't stuff your tweets with hashtags. Sure, you'll wind up in a lot of different hashtagged feeds, but it's super annoying and people will just ignore your tweet.

HOW TO USE AS AN AUTHOR

• **The most important rule:** Don't monetize the conversation. You know how annoying it is when someone tries to sell you something? Yeah. Don't be that person.

• A good rule of thumb that several authors employ is to follow up any tweets about you/your book by talking about someone else's book. Share the good news of others as much as you share good news about yourself.

• Don't approach Twitter like it's a stage. It's not somewhere to shout about books and yourself. Remember the cocktail party: no one wants to talk to someone with no variety.

- Brevity is the soul of wit. It takes awhile to get comfortable with saying something fun in 140 characters, but keep trying.

- Be yourself. There are some amazingly funny people who are killing it on Twitter. You don't have to copy them—find your own voice.

- Retweeting means that someone else's tweet is shared by you, showing up in your followers' newsfeeds.

- You can make your Twitter feed into Facebook, so everything you post on Twitter shows up in your Facebook. This is super annoying to most readers.

GIVEAWAYS

Twitter giveaways tend to be "RT to enter" giveaways—you pick a winner from everyone who retweets a certain tweet you set up, which could include a link to your book cover, a specific message, a graphic, etc.

You could also integrate "follow to enter" giveaways to encourage more followers.

Many authors use hashtags to enter contests—everyone who uses a particular hashtag relevant to the book is entered.

QUIRKS AND THINGS TO KEEP IN MIND

There are a lot of readers on Twitter. Decide how you want to interact with them. Some will tweet you links to book reviews. You do not have to read the reviews; you do not have to respond to the reviews. It's perfectly okay for you to ignore them. Sometimes, readers will tweet to you directly and say something really bad about you or your book. It's hugely frustrating, but remember: *People forget that authors are people.*

Many people will include an author's twitter handle in a tweet about the book just because they're trying to be complete. They're thinking of a link, not a person on the other end of the screen. Don't take it too personally, don't think the reader is trying to attack you or bring you down. Just ignore it.

Sometimes, some readers will be intentionally mean and try to bait you or get a response to negative comments. Block and ignore.

WARNING! WARNING! WARNING!

• Don't use Twitter to attack other readers, such as: "This @reviewer said bad things about my book! Readers, tell her why she's wrong!"

• Don't use Twitter in place of private conversations. Yes, you can @-reply friends and have conversations—but be aware that everyone can read them. They're not private.

• Don't respond to negativity. Don't feed the trolls.

• Remember that everything you say on Twitter is public. Don't say anything you wouldn't mind everyone reading.

• Don't send an auto-DM to everyone who follows you. That's so annoying, and will result in you getting blocked for spam. You also really don't need to thank everyone who follows you. This isn't an invitation from the queen; it's just Twitter.

Tumblr

TUMBLR IS HARD TO EXPLAIN. It's a massive beast of different kinds of blogs, from fandoms to social justice, but many people have "random" blogs that feature things that the blogger likes with a variety of topics. "Booklr" is the book-loving (and often book-reviewing) branch of Tumblr. In Tumblr, you have a dashboard. From the dashboard, you see posts from everyone you follow. Think of it like Twitter, but with longer posts and lots of pictures and .gifs. If you like something, you can click on a little heart to like it. This does nothing but add to your list of things you like, and lets the person who posted it know you liked it. You can also reblog. That's sort of like retweeting—it shows up on your dash and the dash of everyone that follows you.

Link: http://tumblr.com

SETTING UP YOUR PROFILE

Tumblr users will tend to see your posts in their feed, but you should still pay attention to the way your actual blog looks, making sure it's readable and professional looking. For the love of all that's holy, don't use automatic sounds on your blog (such as sound effects when you hover over links or a song that plays as soon as you open the page).

There are lots of free templates available, and in general, those will serve the needs of most authors. You can customize the templates by adding your book cover and additional links (including static pages) to your Tumblr blog. Pay close attention to which photo you use for your avatar—more people will see it than your actual blog. Also, make sure to go into your settings and look at the way your blog will look on a mobile phone; with most themes, you have the chance to add an additional header to feature your books on the mobile version.

THE BASICS

You have several different options of things to post:

• *Text*: Text and photo posts are the most common types of posting on Tumblr. You can write text (with or without a title), and embed links and photos inside the text. Long text may end up being shortened to a link in reblogs.

• *Photo*: A photo post will display the photo(s) first. You can add a caption and text under the photos.

• *Quote*: Quotes tend to show up a little bigger than text posts, and are automatically formatted with quote marks and a spot for citation (which can be linked).

• *Link*: A link will display the link at the top of the post. You can customize what the link says and the text beneath. Longer text posts may end up being abbreviated to links in your blog.

• *Chat*: Chats are formatted differently, displaying a conversation like a script.

• *Audio & Video*: These embed multimedia and can include text and photos underneath.

A Tumblr post can be any length, but shorter is better. If you're writing something long, consider adding a "read more" link so that you don't take up so much room on your followers' newsfeeds.

Many authors add an "ask box" to their page, which enables people to send a question straight to you. You can choose if you allow anonymous posters. All anonymous replies are posted on your blog; non-anonymous replies can be sent privately.

The culture of Tumblr is built on reblogging: you can easily hit "reblog" at the bottom of a post, and that post goes on your Tumblr blog and in your followers' newsfeeds. Reblogging is like retweeting.

You can easily feed your Tumblr posts into Twitter or Facebook—but don't do it for every post you make. Be selective, sharing only a limited number of things on both platforms, and make sure to edit what is displayed on Twitter, rather than the default text.

You can add tags to each post, which will then be searchable across all of Tumblr. Feel free to add as many as you want—they're unobtrusive to readers—but be aware that only the first five will show up in searches, so load your most important tags in the front. You can also use tags to sort and organize your own blog, making it easier for you and readers to find certain posts; therefore, it makes sense to tag posts dealing directly with your books.

HOW TO USE AS AN AUTHOR

As with all social media, don't flood your followers' newsfeeds with constant talk about yourself and your book.

• Give credit. If you take something off the internet, ask permission and give credit to the artist. If you quote something, source it.

• Follow tags—I personally find it worthwhile to follow my author name, "Beth Revis," as well as my Tumblr user name "bethrevis," and the title of my latest book. You'll find reviews—read or not, at your own discretion—but you'll also find quotes, fan art, and fan edits that you can reblog.

You can also search tags for things that interest you, so you can find blogs to follow.

• Tumblr is mostly about community and entertainment. Don't try to sell them something. They won't like it. But if you build a community of people and fandoms that you like, then occasionally post something on your stuff, you're integrating your likes with theirs. It's like this: if you're in line to see the next Harry Potter film, and you start talking to someone else in that line, then you can be reasonably sure they might also like some other book/movie that you like. Therefore, I post about *Firefly* and *Doctor Who* and astronomy and nerdy stuff that I like. People follow me for that. Occasionally, I also post about my book. I figure if people like the other stuff I post, they might like my book.

• Remember: keep it short. Keep it simple. Just a photograph is fine. Just a quote is fine. Just a short paragraph is fine. A three-page essay? Not fine (unless you give a "read more" link).

GIVEAWAYS

The most common style of giveaway is a "reblog to enter" giveaway—you design the post, and anyone who reblogs is entered, sometimes with the corollary that they have to also follow you.

You can also use tags; for example, if you want to encourage people to post fan art or their favorite quotes of your book, have them tag with a specific phrase so you can find it and enter them in the contest.

QUIRKS AND THINGS TO KEEP IN MIND

The same caveats with Twitter exist for Tumblr—don't get involved in review drama. If you want to reblog a review, you can, but don't argue with reviewers; don't do anything more than share it. People will tag you in negative things; don't engage.

Tumblr also tends to be a place that can get very political. Feel free to get involved if you want, but do so with the awareness that politics are extraordinarily controversial, and some people will view you more as a media person than as a person with opinions.

WARNING! WARNING! WARNING!

• Don't add dismissive or aggressive comments to other people's posts, particularly if you're commenting on a reader or reviewer. As the author, the reviewer's opinion of your book is *their* opinion, and you don't need to intrude on it. Don't even be snarky in comments. Be an adult and be professional.

• Remember that everything you post is public; even if you send a message to someone else, they can reply publicly instead of privately.

• You don't have to reply to every ask, particularly anonymous asks, which can be very baiting and rude. It's totally fine to just ignore and delete.

Instagram

INSTAGRAM IS STILL VERY UNDERSERVED in social media, but it's delightful and super easy to use. Basically, think of Instagram as Twitter, except with pictures instead of words. You post pictures, they show up in your followers' feeds. Instagram also makes it easy to post pictures to Facebook (on your personal profile, not your public page), Twitter, and Tumblr.

Link: http://instagram.com, but be aware that to use this program to its full potential, you should download the app on your phone. There *is* a website for it, but it doesn't have all the features of the app, and you need the app for posting.

SETTING UP YOUR PROFILE

Instagram set-up should be done from the phone app. The only links you'll be able to post will be in your profile (any links in captions to pictures aren't clickable), so make sure you're clear about who you are and what you do.

THE BASICS

• Instagram is super easy—just post pictures! You can also add a caption and use tags similar to other social media.

• You can add filters to your pictures, but don't over filter. Use sparingly.

• You can easily feed Instagram to Twitter, Tumblr, and Facebook (although only to your profile, not your page). Be selective on this, but since these platforms adapt well to the Instagram set-up, Instagram is the one social media I think adapts well to being fed across platforms.

HOW TO USE AS AN AUTHOR

Try to post pictures that would be interesting to your readers. These don't always have to be about books—people love seeing a slice of your life—but be aware of what people are seeing, and if you want to make part of your life exposed to the public. Also be aware that not everyone will like things that are too personal—pictures of puppies and cats tend to be universally loved; picture of babies and children, not so much.

When starting out with Instagram, a lot of people worry about what to post. Some good ideas include:

• A picture of a book you're currently reading
• Pictures of your office space/bookshelves
• Pictures of areas where your book is set
• Pictures of author events (not limited to your own!)
• Pictures of fun things you do
• When in doubt: puppies and cats

Instagram is a visual medium that feeds well across platforms. This makes it ideal to develop marketing images specifically for your book. A common one is to make a graphic that uses a quote from your book; this graphic then becomes a teaser for your work.

GIVEAWAYS

Instagram giveaways could include using a hashtag, having people repost a contest picture, or tagging friends in an original post.

QUIRKS & THINGS TO KEEP IN MIND

While you should always be conscious of your privacy and safety, Instagram, by its very nature, makes it easy to share exactly where you are. Twice now I've posted a picture of a place where I was—a coffee shop, a bookstore—and people who follow me on social media showed up in real life. Both times have been very sweet, innocent reactions of teens who recognized my location from the picture and just came over to introduce themselves and talk books, but be aware that if you'd rather remain a little anonymous, you may want to post a picture *after* you've left the area.

WARNING! WARNING! WARNING!

• Don't post pictures that are inappropriate; this should go without saying.

• The same caveats about responding to readers (who can tag you in their pictures) in a negative way.

Facebook

FACEBOOK IS THE OLD STANDBY—everyone has it, even your grandma. Facebook is most often used for personal reasons, to keep up with family members and friends, but there's a place for author pages as well, and it can be used to great effect.

Link: http://facebook.com

SETTING UP YOUR ~~PROFILE~~ *PAGE*

Nearly everyone has a Facebook profile, and it's super easy to set up, but I argue that if you're an author, you need a *page*, not a *profile.* A profile is the first thing you have to set up, and what most people have. Some authors only have a profile—which means their fans "friend" them (as opposed to a page, where fans "like" them). There are a few valid reasons to only have a profile—you skip the added step to set up a page, you may not want to turn a reader-author relationship into a "fan" relationship, you may be worried you won't get likes/fans.

But there are a lot of reasons why this isn't a good idea, particularly if you use your Facebook profile for anything personal, or are friends with anyone in your personal life on your profile.

There is a limit to how many people can friend you in your profile, but no limit to how many people can like your page. You may not have thousands of followers now, but you're looking a lifetime of readers, right? Prepare for them.

A profile page has things specifically designed to help you reach your readers. You can add a "buy my books" link, information about your books, widgets for newsletter sign ups, etc. You can also make this space completely about you and your books, as opposed to splitting it between personal and professional.

You can group friends, and then post only to certain groups. But this is far more complicated and time consuming than just directing readers to a fan page as opposed to your personal profile.

A page creates a layer of removal from you and your fans. I know, your readers are great, but do you really want them looking at pictures of your kids or knowing where you went to dinner with your friends? Even if you control what *you* post, your friends and family can post things and tag you—which can easily end up on your fans' newsfeeds.

You can—and should—select the setting to approve anything you're tagged in. This is the only way to reasonably help ensure that no one else can see things you're tagged in by other people.

A fan page is more professional. It just is. You're doing this for professional purposes, don't mix it up with your personal life. Even if you choose to talk about personal things on your fan page, it's still better to have a professional, removed space in which to do it.

I don't care what level of success you're at, at the end of the day, many of the people who read your book are strangers, and some strangers are creepy, yo. You don't have to be mega famous to get a stalker. This is basic protection of your life—online and off. This distance is *good*.

The primary reason why most people are on Facebook is to connect with people they know personally—family and friends. As much as you love your readers, they are not your family and friends. It's kind of creepy to see them in your timeline.

Facebook security settings are constantly changing, and frankly, are a mess. Your profile settings may change, revealing things about you to your

Facebook friends that you might not want public. But a page setting is by nature more secure and removed.

In short, if you're an author, no matter what your following, and you want a Facebook presence, get a page to direct readers to, not just a profile. Be vigilant, and direct readers to the page, and only family and friends to the profile. Create that distinction in your life—for your own sanity and security, and to save yourself the hassle of separating them later on.

THE BASICS

In a page, you post just like you would in a profile. In general, though, try to use more photos and links than you would in a personal post—they show up more prominently in people's feeds.

Be aware when linking to other authors' pages that you should link to their *page*, not their *profile*. It's just courtesy and maintains their privacy.

While it's fine to do some "like if you agree" or "comment with your thoughts" on posts, be wary of doing that for *every* post.

Make your avatar for your page different from your avatar for your profile. For years, I used my dog's picture for my private profile, to discourage readers from trying to friend my private profile instead of liking my public page. Even if you still use a picture of yourself, use two different pictures to separate your private and professional life. This will also help you not accidentally post something on the wrong space.

Absolutely take advantage of posting events information through Facebook—many people use that feature, even for online events.

Use the photo feature not only to showcase your events, but also to post promotional marketing spaces and alternate versions of your book cover (with your publisher's permission).

HOW TO USE AS AN AUTHOR

Make sure your header image features you or your books in a way that readers can see quickly.

Your page will also feature a "call to action" button that you can alter to provide a link to buy your book, a sign-up form for your newsletter, etc.

Facebook has integrated apps that may be helpful. For example, MailChimp allows you to have a Facebook app that integrates signups straight from your page. Explore them and use the ones that best suit you.

Remember, even though this is a "fan page," don't make it all about you all the time. Feel free to post things that would interest your readers that aren't directly related to your book. Interaction is good; good interaction leads to sales more than a constant bombardment of "buy me!"

Facebook's algorithms and policies are always on the change (frustratingly so). Increasingly, Facebook is making it harder for people who run a page to actually reach the readers that want to hear news. Good interaction—comments, likes, etc.—will help boost your exposure.

Should you pay for more exposure? It's up to you—in general, only boost posts with a paid program if they're truly important (such as a release day post), if then. Whatever you do, though, don't use a shady service to pay for more followers. That is never good, leads to false likes, and reduces your chances of exposure in the future.

GIVEAWAYS

Make sure you know Facebook's policies before you hold any contest or giveaway there; those policies change frequently and could lead to your page getting shut down if you violate them.

Because of Facebook's algorithms, it can be hard for a post to gain footing. One way to do that is to encourage comments and likes. You could offer an entry to people who tag a friend in a comment—that not only means you get a comment, but you typically get a friend (who may not have been aware of your post before) to see and potentially like or comment on it.

QUIRKS & THINGS TO KEEP IN MIND

Facebook makes it crazy easy to feed all other social media into your page—such as every tweet, every blog post, every Tumblr post, every everything.

People aren't here for that. People are here for you on Facebook, not on every other platform. If you don't want to deal with having a Facebook page, don't, but don't just insult your readers by using Facebook as a depository for every other form of social media.

WARNING! WARNING! WARNING!

• Keep apprised of Facebook's policies and security settings; they're notoriously fickle and are something you shouldn't let slip.

• Don't mix up your private life and professional life. Your baby's cute, but readers care more about your book.

• Try not to overload your page with too many apps; focus on what's really important to you. Same goes with feeds.

Pinterest

PINTEREST IS A COMBINATION OF Instagram and microblogging—it relies on a photographs to gain interest. People set up different boards, grouped by interest, and people can follow either a specific board, or everything that a user posts.

Link: http://pinterest.com

SETTING UP YOUR PROFILE

Pinterest will allow you to have a custom profile and avatar, as well as one link in your profile.

THE BASICS

I find it easiest to start with an idea of the kinds of things you want to post. Set up a different board for each type of thing. For example, my authorly boards include:

- Fan art
- Events & Online Programs
- Book covers
- Images that remind me of my books
- Storyboards of books I'm working on
- Inspirational quotes

- Book art

…And so on. Follow other people, or link to things you've found online to create different pins.

You can also encourage people to pin things from your website or blog by adding a "pin it" button. Remember that pins require images, so it's helpful to include a graphic with a post if you want it to be on Pinterest.

HOW TO USE AS AN AUTHOR

Pin things specifically relevant to your books, as well as things that just inspire or remind you of your stories.

Encourage fans to pin images of themselves with your books, to pin pictures of actors for fan casting, etc.

I'm particularly partial to using Pinterest to showcase fan art. By its nature, it includes a link back to the original source (which is hugely important), and you're able to make a widget that displays the pins on your website.

You can also add other people to pin things to your boards, so you could do a group board, or a co-authored board.

QUIRKS & THINGS TO KEEP IN MIND

When repinning, make sure that the original source is still attached to the photo. Pinterest can also easily feed into other social media, but use that feature sparingly.

WARNING! WARNING! WARNING!

A lot of authors use Pinterest to set up storyboards for forthcoming books. But…I want to give a friendly word of warning to this. Sometimes, books don't sell. Sometimes your entire vision changes. Even if you're just posting vague inspirational pictures of your book on Pinterest, there's a chance you'll end up never writing or publishing this book. But readers will have seen the board. They'll bring it up. They'll ask if your next book matches the board. I'm speaking from experience when I say: Keep the book (and its storyboard) very private until it's guaranteed to be a book—not just when the contract is signed, but when it's coming out in a few months and only an act of God would stop it.

Wattpad

WATTPAD IS A SOCIAL MEDIA outlet developed specifically for readers and writers. You post novels or short stories (one section at a time), and interact with other writers and readers through comments.

Link: http://wattpad.com

SETTING UP YOUR PROFILE

Wattpad includes a place for your biography, including a header image, avatar image, and links. You can add links to your individual books directly within your bio page.

THE BASICS

When posting work, you should absolutely have a custom cover and a short description. You can skip both these steps, but your work will suffer for it.

In your description, be clear about your schedule of posting (even if you intend to post sporadically). Also be clear on whether or not you're posting the whole book or just a sample.

Be aware that Wattpad users greatly prefer reading the whole book rather than a sample, and you will anger some readers if you only post a sample. The best policy is just to be upfront about it from the start, and not blindside readers with a "to read the whole thing, buy the book" notice at the end.

Your rank goes up if you have more "reads." Each time a person logs on to read a different section of your book, that counts as a "read." This means that if you only have one section of your work (such as a short story that's posted all at once) and have a hundred reads, then a hundred people read it. But if you split up your story into two sections, and have a hundred reads, then fifty people read part one and then read part two (or seventy-five people read part one and only twenty-five people read part two, etc.). If a hundred people read both sections, you have two hundred Wattpad "reads."

People can also "vote" for your work by giving it a star, which is similar to saying that they like what you've written.

Readers can comment on a section, on the book as a whole, and even on specific lines of text. Wattpad greatly encourages interaction with authors, so be aware that your works will likely receive far more comments here than in other mediums.

Readers can send you private messages as well.

HOW TO USE AS AN AUTHOR

Sample chapters: Many published authors post just sample chapters of their work on Wattpad. If you're traditionally published, make sure you ask your publisher how much of your novel you can post (typically only three to five chapters). Self published people can decide how much they want to post on their own, unless they're enrolled in Kindle Select, which limits the percentage of work that can be shared anywhere outside of Amazon.

Full stories and novellas: If you have short stories or novellas that you can share and don't mind adding them for free, by all means post on Wattpad. Even if the entire story/novella is done, consider breaking it up into smaller sections and posting on a schedule to build anticipation and grow your audience.

Full novels: If you're self published, or if your publisher has let the rights revert back to you, you're free to publish the whole novel on Wattpad. Some people believe this will generate sales to sequels, some people care more about exposure than sales. Keep in mind that if you post your whole book for free on Wattpad, Amazon will price match and make your book free on their site as well.

"Read for read": Many users of Wattpad swap reads, and may offer to read your work if you read theirs, or they may simply ask you to read and comment on your work in a critique fashion. Feel free to do this if you want to, but doing so can become overwhelming fast. You are not obligated to participate.

GIVEAWAYS

A few authors have used Wattpad as a place to gather short stories for a contest, usually as an entry method for a larger prize run by their publisher. This can be a very daunting task, though, and it's something you should research carefully before you do it.

QUIRKS & THINGS TO KEEP IN MIND

When authors sign up for Wattpad, the first thing they ask is, "How do I get readers to look at my work?"

And soon after that, they say, "How can this translate to sales?"

The short answer is: They don't.

It's true that for some people, posting a sample of a book with a link to where to buy the book, or posting a whole book with a link to buy the series, may result in a significant boost in sales. This is, however, by and large the exception to the rule.

Wattpad readers tend to be an insular community. They comprise mostly of teenagers, and therefore they don't have much expendable cash. Instead, they read heavily on Wattpad, where everything is free and has the added bonus of a community and interaction.

This is *not* a bad thing. These readers are passionate and the comments are typically awesome. And readers are always good—the exposure could lead to indirect sales. There are a few cases of Wattpad stories leading to traditional book sales, and you can always use your Wattpad statistics to help advertise your book

But if you expect your hundred thousand reads on Wattpad to equal a hundred thousand sales…that's probably not going to happen. If you expect a hundred thousand reads to equal a hundred sales…that *may* happen, and may not.

Rather than trying to monetize Wattpad, embrace it for what it is: A community of readers that tends to stay within the community.

WARNING! WARNING! WARNING!

Get your publisher's okay to post any part of your sold novel on Wattpad, and discuss with your agent whether or not it's better to post a short story on Wattpad or to try to sell it to an anthology.

You're likely going to be asked to read other people's writings, often teens, as that is such a huge part of Wattpad's audience. Use wisdom in this situation. You want to be helpful, but you can get inundated with read requests very quickly. And you need to consider if you're the best person to advise a teen's writing; you don't know the teen personally and can't know if they'd respond better to positive encouragement or constructive criticism.

GoodReads

GOODREADS IS A PLACE FOR readers—it's a book reviewing sight. Because of that, it is not the ideal place for authors. Many authors completely eschew GoodReads, and if you know you can't handle looking at reviews of your own book, consider avoiding this outlet altogether.

Link: http://goodreads.com

SETTING UP YOUR PROFILE

GoodReads does have a place for authors, and even if you don't intend to ever truly participate in the site, you may want to set your profile up. Doing this will add a note that you're a "GoodReads Author" on your biography page, and it enables you to control what is displayed on your biography page, including:

• Selecting the picture you want to display

• Selecting how much personal information (your location, gender, etc.) you want to display

• Providing a link to your website

• Providing your genres

• Writing your own biography

Without setting up an author profile, the default biography for you may be very sparse, and the information may be gleaned by others from outside sources.

THE BASICS

In GoodReads, you'll get an author dashboard. At the top, you'll see a display of your statistics, including average ranking and number of ratings, followed by a breakdown of ranks/ratings and other stats per book.

You can also set up an "Ask the Author" feature that enables people to ask things of you and you to answer easily. The answers are compiled in your biography page.

If you're a self published author, you can set up your book's page and information on your own; if you're traditionally published, your publisher may do this for you. Discuss with them first before you upload anything; they may intend to do a bigger cover or description reveal.

Note: "Librarians" are like moderators, and they can make more changes to pages than an author or average user can. If you have trouble, you can request a change from a librarian.

GoodReads users are notoriously on the ball about tracking down information about books. If there's something you're trying to keep secret—for example a book cover—keep an eye on GoodReads to see if it's posted early and alert your publisher if that happens.

HOW TO USE AS AN AUTHOR

DO NOT RESPOND TO REVIEWS. There is never a time when this is okay. Even positive responses are not well received. This is a *reader space*, not an author space, so do not invade their space. People come to GoodReads for honest discussions of books, and just knowing the author is there, watching them (even if it's in a positive way, such as to thank them for the review), makes it awkward at best and threatening at worse. Unlike other social media, where interaction with fans is encouraged, GoodReads is a place for criticism and readers exclusively, and the author should never intrude.

If you can't handle reading reviews, **DO NOT READ REVIEWS.** If you can handle reading reviews, by all means, see what other people are saying. But if reading negative reviews causes you depression or makes you want to lash out at reviewers, *don't read the reviews.*

Should you add your own reviews of other books? This is an often-debated topic among authors, but my personal stance is: No. Don't review. There are several reasons for this. First and foremost, you will obviously not love every book you ever read, but you don't want to insult your peers and friends. Second, if you only post positive reviews, not only does that make you seem like you are a shallow reader, but it will be a red flag to reader friends who know you've read their book but haven't posted a review. In the end, do what you feel comfortable doing, but be aware that many authors will not like seeing their works reviewed by peers. My personal policy is only to give five-star reviews to books I've actually blurbed, and the review is restricted to the wording on the blurb.

An argument for adding reviews to GoodReads is that it gives readers a sense of your style and what books you like (and don't). If your reading preferences are close to theirs, they may be more willing to take a chance on buying and reading your book. But you need to be aware that you can turn people away by your reviews and burn bridges with other authors.

You can also add the GoodReads widget, with links to your books, to your other online media, such as your website.

GoodReads links are often a very easy, impartial link to use when you're discussing yours or other books online. Because it doesn't link to a single retailer but does have links to all retailers, it's easier to share. However, since Amazon acquired GoodReads, some authors are more hesitant to use it.

GoodReads communities are similar to forums. Some welcome authors, some are author-free; make sure you understand what type of conversation you're participating in. GoodReads can be a great place to host a Q&A or book club style discussion, but much like you can't entirely be honest about a book if the author is sitting right in front of you, many people will prefer book discussions to be closed to the author.

Don't rate your own books. It's tacky. I mean, it doesn't hurt anything, and of course you believe your book deserves five stars, but in general, there's really no point in it. Some people use a review of their own books as a place to showcase awards (such as a Kirkus star) and professional reviews, or to discuss what they were trying to do with their book, but again, use this tactic at your own carefully considered discretion. If you want to talk a little about the inspiration or background of your book in your own review of your book, that's far better than giving yourself five stars and smiley face.

GIVEAWAYS

It's very easy to set up a giveaway for your book on GoodReads, and having a giveaway here is something that should be a part of most marketing plans. Most traditional publishers will set this up, but it's something you can so as an author of self publisher easily as well.

GoodReads also offers paid advertisements, much like Facebook, but with an obviously more targeted reading audience.

Some GoodReads communities are structured around author promotion. You'll need to look around to find some that fit your needs.

QUIRKS & THINGS TO KEEP IN MIND

People can rate and review your book as soon as the book's page is live—including giving your book that's not even written a one-star review. Don't sweat it. People use GoodReads in many different ways—some people use star ranking as a way to remember how much they want a book (in which case, a one-star could be a number one choice for them, and a reminder to buy it when its available).

WARNING! WARNING! WARNING!

GoodReads can be dangerous grounds for many readers, particularly those who don't react well to their own reviews. You don't have to be on GoodReads ever. Period. Whatever you do, don't respond to reviews. Even if you think the review is unfair, even if it's factually wrong, whatever—it's not the place for you to join the conversation.

That said, if a review is personally threatening or inappropriate in a way that libelous, of course contact GoodReads and report the review. Don't engage the reviewer yourself, just report it.

Don't spam readers. Please, don't do this. On GoodReads, people can add you as a friend. I—and most authors—will friend everyone who requests it. Friends can then send messages to readers. If you're an author, don't send a message to readers that says "thanks for adding me as a GoodReads friend." It's trite and pointless. And for the love of Pete, don't ever send a "please read or add my books!" message to readers. Just don't. That's spam, that's annoying, and that gets you blocked. Don't try to dress it up, either, by complimenting the reader on her taste or by making it seem like an exclusive offer. Don't belittle yourself, begging for a moment of the reader's time. It's still spam, it's still annoying, and it will still get you blocked.

YouTube

YOUTUBE IS FOR VIDEOS. While originally dominated by vloggers, today it offers short films, series, trailers, and much more.

Link: http://youtube.com

SETTING UP YOUR PROFILE

YouTube is now linked to Google, so your same user name on Google applies. You can set up a channel where you can post videos and personalize it.

THE BASICS

The hard part is going to be to make the videos, not upload them to YouTube. YouTube is very easy to use, both in uploading and sharing videos, but creating the content for YouTube takes a whole different skillset.

Some people do very well by just looking into the camera and talking, which is what a true vlog is. Some people develop content that's scripted and directed, from a book trailer to more complex works that links to their books.

A good middle ground is to use YouTube to show readers details about your books that you couldn't otherwise do. If your book is set in a specific city, explore that city with your video camera. If you have a lot of commentary you want to add to your book, stage an interview that you can upload and share with readers. Think about what sort of content you can add that people would want to see and hear, as oppose to read about.

HOW TO USE AS AN AUTHOR

Decide on what you want to say—you may want a vlog-style channel with regular posts of you talking at the camera, you may want to reserve your channel for scripted material like book trailers, or a mix of both.

Even if you don't intend to do regular recordings on YouTube, it's worthwhile to have a channel. You can post a vlog just at your book's release, you can use YouTube to give a thank you shout-out to readers, you can post interviews of yourself (either with questions you wrote or with questions you accept from readers), etc.

While many authors don't use YouTube, many readers do—book reviews in vlog form are increasingly popular, as are "unboxing" of books, fan-made trailers, etc.

QUIRKS & THINGS TO KEEP IN MIND

Be aware that what you watch, like, and comment on under your user name will likely show up in your profile.

WARNING! WARNING! WARNING!

Just because you're simply talking to a camera doesn't mean you don't need to edit your work down. Become familiar with video editing programs. Even if a work is "live," you could always script bullet points or even write out what you want to say before you go on camera.

Err on the side of short. Most people don't want to spend more than five minutes watching any online video, unless that video is essentially movie-quality. Break up longer programs into sessions released over time if you have a lot to say.

Blogs

A BLOG IS A PLACE FOR LONGER ARTICLES, organized by date, on a website that's typically designed for blog use. Some people have completely abandoned long-form blogging in place of micro-blogging, typically via Twitter or Tumblr.

Link: Various platforms; the most popular are Blogger (http://blogger.com) and WordPress (http://wordpress.com).

Your blog should be as professionally presented as your website, including the design—in fact, if you can integrate your blog into your website, that's even better. Both Blogger and WordPress can do this; Blogger via "Pages" and WordPress via a built-in blogging design. If your website design can't match (mine doesn't), consider using the same header on both to keep it all tied together.

Appearance also includes the appearance of individual posts. Include pictures to break up text, avoid using hard-to-read fonts or a black background with white or red text. (Note: black and red are one of the most common forms of color-blindness; if you have a black background with red text or vice versa, some of your audience will never be able to read your site.)

Even if you have this information on your website, include your contact information and book information on your blog. Some people who Google your name will go straight to your blog without ever clicking on your website, making it important to spread the info to both places.

The previous prevailing advice on blogs was to have a steady schedule and post regularly. This advice is now outdated. People don't tend to visit a blog regularly; instead, they visit their social media regularly, and click on blogs that are linked there. For that reason, feeding your blog through your social media is important, particularly if you stage the information rather than just using an automatic feed. A social media link to your blog whenever you post it is far more important than keeping a schedule and routine of posting.

Most people move discussions of an article into social media rather than discussing via comments. A tweet is the new comment. You will likely not generate that many comments on blog posts, but that's fine—people are likely talking about the article on their social media platforms rather than on the article page itself. If someone shares a link on Twitter or other social media platforms, that's far more beneficial that a comment on the blog post.

Blog content has changed as well. Some blogs maintain a constant focus on one subject, such as writing advice, and they create a niche for themselves in that market. Most authors, however, are more focused on their own careers in their blogs rather than on monetizing a specific feature. Therefore, many author blogs may mention not just craft advice, but also event information, book release details, and more. Whether you want to focus on a niche or make a more general idea of your writing life for your content is fine—both have worked well for different authors in the past.

Blogs—particularly those of authors—tend to be far less stuffy and formal than they previously were. Many readers go to blogs now to get an idea of what a reader's personality is, and they expect a tone similar to the more casual tone of social media. You don't have to put on a suit to write a blog; feel free to be yourself.

Personally, I've greatly reduced my blogging output. I've done this for several reasons, but primarily it was for survival. You have to make choices on where you spend your time, and it was more beneficial (and fun) for me to use social media than a blog. That said, I still maintain my blog, not just for the archives, but for whenever I want to write an essay or a longer post that wouldn't fit with other social media forms. Blogs also create a good "home base" for contests—when you host a contest, put the main post on your blog and link out to social media from there.

One word of warning: When readers Google you, they're most likely to click on either your static website or your blog. If your last blogpost is insanely dated, it looks a bit lame. If you know you're not going to update your blog often, perhaps add a static post on top directing readers to where you and/or your books are. Periodically Google yourself, just to see what others see when they look for you. If they first link you come across is a blog with a post dated three years ago that's all about a book that was never published, delete or update that blog to something that readers will find beneficial.

False Likes & Followers

WHEN YOU START OUT ON SOCIAL MEDIA, the most depressing thing is to look at your follower count and notice just how nonexistent it is. It takes time to grow a following on social media, and while there *are* short cuts, they're not advisable. There's an entire subset of individuals on social media who think that having a lot of followers or likes is imperative for success, but they're putting the cart before the horse. It's not that you get successful because you have a lot of likes or follows; you get a lot of likes and follow *because* you're successful.

BUYING LIKES AND FOLLOWS

Don't ever do this.

In *no* case is this advisable.

Inflating your numbers falsely doesn't help you. It reduces your overall reach (particularly in Facebook), it's a waste of money, and it does nothing but puff up your ego. It's a waste of time and money, and a desperate plea for attention.

Don't ever do this.

LIKE-FOR-LIFE & FOLLOW-FOR-FOLLOW CAMPAIGNS

Don't ever do this.

In *no* case is this advisable.

Trading likes and follows is pointless. Sure, you can get tens of thousands of twitter followers, but to what end? You're talking to a vacuum of people who only followed you so you'd follow them. No one's benefitting here. It's such a waste of time, and anyone who understands social media will look at your high follower rate combined with your high follows rate and know that you're so desperate to be liked that you're basically begging and bribing people to click a button on your profile.

Don't do this.

HOW TO GET FOLLOWERS

Be a part of your community.

Participate in conversations.

Occasionally hold contests to encourage people to follow you and spread the word about your social media. *Example:* "RT this message and follow me for a chance to win this book!" These campaigns should be done sparingly, but can be effective means to exposure.

Include your social media information and follow links wherever you are online, if appropriate. Add it to your email signature, put it on your website, include in your footer information when you post on forums.

Wait. It takes time. If you're just now signing up to Twitter, don't expect ten thousand followers in a week. Or a month. Or even a year.

Build an authentic community based on real people having a real dialogue about books and writing and your other interests.

There is no shortcut to building relationships.

Some Social Media Strategies

THE FOLLOWING ARE SOME POSSIBLE approaches to social media. They're certainly not the only way, and they're just some jumping off points to consider.

Goal: Garner attention for a new book

Timeline: One month before publication + one week following publication

Platforms: Instagram (with optional feeds to Twitter & Facebook), Blog (either a formal blog or Tumblr), Newsletter

Strategy: Develop teaser graphics with a quote or tagline, the book's cover (or part of the cover), and the release date. Starting one month before publication, post the graphics on Instagram, spacing them out to end about one week after release.

Post several blog posts about the inspiration, background, process of writing, etc., of your novel. Always include a copy of the book cover, links to pre-orders, and maybe even a tagline or quote from the book in each post. Use other social media platforms to publicize the posts. Space these out to cover the entire timeframe.

Develop a contest for a giveaway of your book (signed) and some other goodies, using platforms to advertise. Stage the giveaway to end a day before your book's release, and follow the winner announcement with, "If you didn't win, you still have time to order a copy of the book here!"

One week before release, send out a newsletter to subscribers. Use your blog posts as links of interest for the newsletter, and add details about the giveaway. Obviously make sure your book and it's buy-links are prominently placed.

On release day, post on Instagram, your blog, and any other social media feeds, emphasizing that the book is out now.

Optional: On release day, have a "launch party" using your preferred method of social media (i.e. a twitter hashtag chat, a Facebook party, etc.).

Goal: Garner attention for a sequel

Timeline: Three months before publication + one week following publication

Platforms: Instagram (with optional feeds to Twitter & Facebook), Blog (either a formal blog or Tumblr), Newsletter

Strategy: Use a similar strategy to launching a new book.

Stage three giveaways, one per month before release. Each should get progressively larger. The first can be just an ARC of the sequel, the second could be a signed copy of both Book 1 and sequels, the third could be signed copies of all books and something else that ties with the books.

Each giveaway also involves a different level of reader involvement in social media, increasing as the prize gets better. The first one could require nothing more than a simple share of a tweet or Facebook post, the second steps it up to include a specific message, and the third could be based on fan art contributions or pictures posts of people with copies of your book(s).

Goal: Maintain a social presence with limited time

Timeline: Monthly

Platforms: Blog, Newsletter

Strategy: Develop 1-2 interesting blog posts per month. Alternatively, curate a handful of interesting topics from the internet that are relevant to your genre.

Create a standard template for a newsletter that allows you to add articles simply and easily.

Each month, release a newsletter which includes the articles and your book's buy information.

Optional: Encourage sign-ups by teasing what upcoming, exclusive information will be presented in your upcoming newsletter on social media. Also mention when your newsletter is available online, along with a message similar to, "Never miss another newsletter, sign up here!"

Goal: Build a presence on a social media platform

Timeline: N/A

Platforms: Select one

Strategy: Pick the social media you'd like to focus on getting more action in.

Follow your peers—people in your genre, other writers, agents, etc.—and learn while you observe.

When you're comfortable with the platform, consider running a few platform-specific contests. Examples: to build Twitter followers, offer a prize for people who retweet a message; to build Tumblr followers, offer a prize for people who reblog.

Be aware that a percentage of people will only follow or share to enter the contest, but it can give you a base to grow upon.

Book Release Marketing

Marketing

Launch your book with these strategies.

Book Trailers

A BOOK TRAILER IS A SHORT video, usually posted on YouTube and used across platforms, advertising the book.

You can see an example of my own book trailer, made by the publisher, at http://bit.ly/ATUtrailer. It's an animated graphic using the book cover of *Across the Universe*, with the audiobook narrator reading a selection from the book. I made my own trailer for *The Body Electric* using stock videography and music, which you can see at http://bit.ly/TBEtrailer. Both links are also available by scanning the QR code in the front of this book.

When it comes to book trailers, they're effectiveness is dubious. A stellar book trailer will garner attention, and they're useful during presentations or to hype a book for a school visit, but if the cost out of pocket to you is more than about a hundred dollars, you likely won't see a return on your investment.

ADVANTAGES OF BOOK TRAILERS

• They are a new medium that's exciting—more dynamic than a still image, a book trailer can provide far more visual appeal.

• They can be used as a preview of the book prior to a book signing or a classroom visit.

• Some people love them and specifically seek them out.

• They're easy to integrate into media presentations; if you're giving a speech at a library, for example, you can use a quick viewing of the book trailer as intermission or a transition into another part of your speech.

• It's not difficult to keep costs down and still create a professional book trailer if one uses stock videography.

DISADVANTAGES OF BOOK TRAILERS

• They can be very expensive if the author has to foot the bill herself and uses custom videography and music.

• Their effectiveness is debatable at best.

• Most readers are unaware of their existence, and will only seek out or bother viewing a trailer if they're already interested in the book. In other words, they don't tend to attract new readers but are something people already fans of your work will view.

• Poorly made book trailers reflect poorly on your work.

TRAITS OF A GOOD BOOK TRAILER

• *They should be short.* A short book trailer is by far better. Shoot for less than a minute. Thirty seconds is better. If you can, get something with ten seconds or so of footage that can easily adapt to social media links (think of the way Vine videos automatically play in social media, and how you can emulate that with your trailer). You could also use a shortened segment for a paid advertisement, for example on Facebook.

• *They should not give away the whole plot.* The point of the trailer is to give a teaser taste of the book, not to give the whole story.

• *They should be more than just words and still pictures.* It's easy to use a video editing service to throw up a few images with a Ken Burns effect overlaid with some words in Impact font. It's so easy, in fact, that this is what many people do . . . even though it's boring and not effective in the least.

• *They should integrate both video and sound.* You may want to have someone narrate dialogue, or you may just want music, but sound is an important feature that shouldn't be forgotten and should coincide with the images.

VARIATIONS OF EFFECTIVE BOOK TRAILERS

• **The mini-movie:** These are formatted like a movie's book trailer, showing a few flashes of scenes, or one specific scene of the book.

• **The tagline only:** The entire trailer is focused on the tagline of the book, all images and text leading up to that one momentous tagline. This could also be focused on a particularly key quote from the book, or a quote that works as a good epithet for the book.

• **The hypothetical:** The trailer shows the choice of the main hero of the novel, and ends with a question, either asking the reader what she'd do in the situation, or just posing the "how can the hero decide?" question.

• **The call to action:** This trailer focuses on the viewer/reader, turning the tables and asking the viewer to discover the truth or challenging the viewer to explore the world of the novel.

• **The character introduction:** With a large cast of characters, showing each one and their defining trait may be enough to introduce readers to the world. Alternatively, you could focus on the love triangle of the book, introducing each person and ending with the hook of "who will she choose?"

ALTERNATIVES TO BOOK TRAILERS

• **Author interview:** An author interview allows you to focus more on the writing process, or on a specific feature of the book. It's also far easier to implement a decent author interview (which requires few, if any, effects) than a decent book trailer, and can be more effective, particularly for the school/library market. You can check out my author interview here: http://bit.ly/ATUinterview.

• **A more unique video:** You don't have to do a traditional book trailer just to get a video of your book online at YouTube. I've seen authors stage flash mobs, a mock music video, and more—and they stand out because they're different. I pitched a video of shooting my sci fi book into space via a weather balloon, and it had great success. See it here: http://bit.ly/ATUspace

• **Let the fans do the work:** Offer a prize for the best fan-made trailer!

Press Kits & One Sheets

SOMETIMES, A PUBLISHER WILL make a press kit or one sheet for you. Press kits are intended for people who want to either request you for an appearance or request your book for review (more along the lines of a major print production review, as opposed to a blogger review). One sheets are often used at conferences or at live events, particularly library or educational conferences, as an introduction to a book or series.

Having both available for download is something that may not be used often, but they're worth having and are relatively simple to make yourself. My press kit has been requested only a handful of times, but each time has paid off in either professional speaking engagements or formal media interviews and reviews. I take my one-sheets to events where there will be a lot of authors presenting in a professional situation; many times, the librarians or teachers may not be in a position to buy a book in that exact moment, but they are inclined to buy an entire classroom set at a different time based on the information provided in the one-sheet.

If your publisher doesn't make these available to you, there's nothing wrong with either asking if they have one on file that you can add to your site or just making your own. If you have to make your own, here are some tips—but definitely go to other author websites and look at what they have for more ideas.

PRESS KIT

The format of the press kit should be clean and readable, but still presented professionally. Avoid using full color backgrounds; this may be something people will want to print and refer to later and don't want to waste a lot of ink on (particularly a teacher who is using your press kit to help write a grant for you to appear at their school). Don't be shy about making the photographs and even some text in color for style purposes, but don't make every page saturated.

For an example of a press kit, go to: http://bethrevis.com/contact/

Elements to include:

• **Opening page**

- Book cover and synopsis of book if a standalone; all book covers and synopsis of series if there's more than one book available currently.

• **Second and subsequent pages, using space as needed**

- Information about the author

- Headshot of the author

- Basic information of the book, including:

> - Format

> - Publisher

> - Publication year (of first book, if this is part of a series)

> - ISBN (of first book, if part of a series)

- Additional information, such as "ebook and audiobooks also available."

- Some top blurbs or reviews of the book

- List of awards and accolades the book has received

- Contact information of the author

- Contact information of the agent for rights purposes

- Any stipulations or costs of appearances

• **End: sample chapter—the first chapter of first book**

ONE SHEET

While it's worthwhile to have a one-sheet available for download, it's far more likely that you'll want print copies of this available at professional conventions you attend or that you can mail to librarians. Whereas you want to make your press kit something that's easily reproducible, you can add more design to your one-sheet, taking it to a print shop prior to use for a professional finish.

The key with a one-sheet is to make it literally one sheet of paper, and one-sided. It needs to be eye-catching and pretty, with enough information to entice someone to look more into purchasing your book. Design is key—make this look good.

For an example of a one sheet, turn the page or go to http://bethrevis.com/contact/

Elements to include:

• A background linked to your books that looks nice

• In clear letters across the top, your book's title or the series title

• The book cover, plus a brief synopsis. If you have a series, include either the first book and synopsis as well as a series synopsis, or all the books in the series with a brief synopsis.

• A short bio and headshot

• Publisher name and ISBN of book

• Some social media links (don't inundate this, but feel free to include the top social media you use)

• Consider adding a QR code or link for more information

• If you can add brief accolades—such as a Kirkus Star—include them

Example One Sheet

ARC Distribution

ADVANCED READER COPIES (ARCs) are valuable in garnering early buzz for your book, as well as reviews.

Traditional publishers print and distribute ARCs to reviews, and provide a certain number of ARCs to the author. Feel free to discuss with your agent or publisher if you need more, especially if you have a specific plan with what to do with them. Also talk with your publisher about what you should do with ARC requests from bloggers and reviewers—some publishers prefer that you forward all emails to them, some suggest you make a list and send to them, some prefer you to just post the publicist's email for people to make direct requests.

Self published authors have the option to not produce ARCs at all, make their own ARCs, or send out electronic ARCs.

But what does an author do with personal copies of ARCs?

GIVEAWAYS

ARCs are a great resource to add to giveaways to help generate buzz. You can design your own giveaway and host on your social media or website, or you can use GoodReads to develop a giveaway.

For a GoodReads giveaway, consult your publisher if you're traditionally published—they may already have one in the works, and you don't want to get in their way. If you do a GoodReads giveaway, obviously make sure you follow their rules and guidelines.

You get to elect when and how long the giveaway runs. There are several different theories on the best ways to do this, but I've found that running a giveaway for 1-2 weeks works best for me.

JOINT GIVEAWAYS

It's also worthwhile to save a few ARCs for different purposes throughout the months immediately before and after your release. Join a group giveaway on social media, provide a signed ARC for a raffle or charity auction, participate in a giveaway meme, etc. If I get ten ARCs, I tend to set aside at least three for random opportunities that may crop up.

LOCAL LIBRARY & BOOKSTORE DISTRIBUTION

Particularly if your title is not being heavily promoted by your publisher, consider dropping off an ARC at your local library or bookstore, especially if you want to do an event there and know that the manager hasn't had a chance to read your ARC. Rather than just mail it to them (where it may get lost in the shuffle), drop it by in person, asking to speak to the manager in charge of your genre or the person in charge of events.

Should you do this if you're self published? It won't hurt, and may get you featured in their local shelves, but keep in mind that it's often very difficult for a bookstore to sell self published works—mainly because most self published books are non-returnable, which is a gamble for bookstores. Many bookstores are using sell-on-commission options to help out local self publishers, though, so it'd be worthwhile to investigate those options. Libraries may be willing to feature a book that's donated, or host an event in their space.

TARGET REVIEWERS

The ultimate goal of ARCs is to generate reviews for the book. It's worthwhile to contact the leading reviewers in your genre to see if they'd be interested in receiving an ARC. If you're traditionally published, reach out to your publicist to find out if there are reviewers they'd like you to contact, or if they'd prefer to handle it themselves.

Be as professional as possible, read and follow the reviewer's guidelines, and only query reviewers who you legitimately think would be a good match for your book—don't just query the ones with big followings. And if you do query a reviewer and they accept the ARC, be aware that it will be your responsibility to ensure the ARC gets to the reviewer (or provide the e-ARC in their preferred format). If you offer the ARC for a review, you provide the ARC—don't expect the reviewer to purchase the book or check it out from the library.

Many traditional publishers will automatically enroll your book into NetGalley or a similar e-ARC distribution site, such as Edelweiss. If you're self published or if you have permission from your traditional publisher, you could also provide the book for e-ARC distribution yourself. By far the cheaper and easier legitimate option is to join a NetGalley co-op; a group of people share the costs and workload of distributing e-ARCs for NetGalley.

BLOG TOURS

Both self publishers and traditional publishers can take advantage of blog tours as a way to gain exposure for their books. More information on those to follow, but keep in mind that if you'd like to have reviews with your blog tour, you'll need to provide an ARC—paper or electronic—to every blogger on the tour. It's not advisable to hope that one ARC gets passed around to each participant; inevitably, one person will forget to mail it off, it'll get lost in the mail, or won't reach all participants in some other way.

Newsletters

I DIDN'T REALLY UNDERSTAND the importance of a newsletter until I self published. The number one thing I was told, over and over again, was simply: Get a newsletter, make it amazing.

The logic is simple. While you may send a tweet out to hundreds or thousands of people, it's a crapshoot on whether or not they actually see it. On the flipside, a newsletter goes directly into their inbox—they'll see at least its presence, whether or not they elect to open it.

When should you start a newsletter? When you have something to say. Start gathering email addresses when you get to the point where you know you are going to publish something, either self or traditionally. Some advice out there says to be aggressive, but I like the slow build. You're looking for your hardcore fans with a newsletter—and everyone has some. It's about quality, not quantity. That said, make it easy for the people who *do* want to get your newsletter to get it with a clear, accessible, easy-to-find sign up form.

Many authors hesitate to do newsletters under the idea of, "I have nothing to say." If you could write one blog post a month, you have something to say— just shift your focus to a newsletter and you're there.

Many other authors hesitate because they're not sure how to get subscribers. It's not that different from building subscriber bases for social media.

Make the sign up link easy to find in multiple places. Periodically post a link to the sign up on social media, something like: "My newsletter goes out tomorrow, and subscribers will learn X! Sign up at http://bit.ly/bethnews." Whenever you mention your newsletter, also include the sign up. Add sign up information on swag. If you're self published, add a sign up link in the back or front matter of your book. Hold giveaways where signing up for your newsletter nets an entry.

Alternatively, you could hold a giveaway for every newsletter—each month, select a subscriber to win a small prize or copy of your book. Self published authors can take advantage of couponing systems to offer all subscribers special coupon codes to their works.

Don't forget to have a sign-up sheet for your newsletter at live events— often my best readers can be found there.

There are a few reliable newsletter services out there, but I currently use MailChimp, which I find to be the easiest program to start with, so all my information here refers to it. Whichever program you end up using, make sure it's reliable, has reasonable rates, and provides easy-to-format newsletters and the option to download the email addresses of your subscribers as a backup.

MailChimp has a very easy sign up form generator that you can personalize to your brand. Mine's at http://bit.ly/bethnews.

Make a custom sign up form, even if it's the simplest design. It makes sign-ups easy for your readers. While you're at it, in that same place where you make a sign up form, make a widget you can embed in your websites. People will come to you in different ways, so be ready to help them sign up in the way they prefer.

I also use bit.ly and get a shortened URL of my sign up form. I prefer it because I can get a custom URL—mine is bit.ly/bethnews. This makes it easier to remember where the sign up form is, so you can easily link it. Composing a tweet? Remind readers of the form. Planning a cover reveal? Form. Random person asks you for a link to the form? It's easy to remember a custom shortened link.

Once you've got sign ups started, you need to develop your newsletter schedule and content.

SCHEDULED VS. SPORADIC NEWSLETTERS

Some people feel the best method of sending out newsletters is on a schedule. Others feel you should only send out a newsletter when you have something important to say, such as when a new book comes out. When deciding which was better for me, I ultimately chose a monthly schedule. My newsletters go out near the beginning of every month—not exactly on the first, but I shoot for the first Monday since I tend to have better interactions on Mondays.

I based my schedule on my own reaction to newsletters. Before working on my own, I signed up for a lot of different authors' newsletters to compare what other people were doing. The ones who sent out on a schedule were ones I came to expect. I didn't open every single one of them, but I didn't mark them as spam, either. The ones that came at bursts I found annoying. One author only sent a newsletter when she had news to share—but then she sent three in two weeks. It was in conjunction with her book launch, and I understood her excitement, but it was annoying and it got to the point where I auto-deleted her newsletters and eventually unsubscribed. I found that, personally, I really didn't want to see a newsletter more than once a month, but I did want that reliable contact of a once a month email.

What's worse is that there are a handful of authors who I was legitimately interested in hearing from . . . and now, more than a year later, they've only sent one newsletter, if that. By that point, I've forgotten about them and their book—in fact, a lot of the times I'd even forgotten that I'd subscribed to them and sent them to the spam folder before realizing my error.

People forget they signed up for your news. You go in the spam filter. You get blocked.

People who sign up for your newsletter want your news—so give it to them.

It's not that hard to gather a month's worth of material into a newsletter, particularly if you design your newsletter to be about more than you. Find a schedule that works for you, and be clear to your readers what that schedule is when they sign up—monthly, bi-monthly, quarterly, etc. Make it a part of your routine, and you'll be surprised just how easy it will be to maintain.

CHATTY VS. INFORMATIVE

People also worry about the tone of their newsletters—should they be friendly or just the facts, ma'am. In all reality, it's up to you. The most logical thing to do is match the style of your books. If you're writing fun, lighthearted books, make your newsletters similar. If your books are more serious in tone, perhaps stick to that style.

In general, shorter is better. In my own newsletters, I use a template that constricts how much information I type, instead opting for "Read More" buttons if people are interested. I have a short opening paragraph—usually just 2-3 sentences—followed by six articles I link to that only have a small paragraph of information before the "Read More" button. This way, people don't have to scan a block of text to get to the good parts—it's right there, abbreviated for them to easily find.

TEMPLATES VS. TEXT

A plain text email may invite a more conversational tone; some authors prefer to have their readers respond as if the newsletter was a personal email directly to them, and they have success that way.

However, templated newsletters look more professional, and they're more likely to be read—or at least scanned. My template has a brief introduction (which includes a quote from one of my books and easy-to-spot buy links), three articles about me (either my latest release, a big upcoming event, or just something directly related to my books), three articles about my genre or reading in general that are of interest to people who read my type of books, a "currently reading" section for me to highlight another author, a "fan art" section for me to highlight an artist, a list of upcoming events, and "bottom material" that never changes—a few short sentences on how to reach me, an ebook coupon, and how to request events. That may seem like a lot, but honestly, because the template is there, it's really not. Making my newsletter becomes a matter of just filling in the blanks of something I've already made before, and it takes me roughly an hour while watching TV to do the entire thing.

Keep an eye on design. I actually paid for the template design I use—$18. Not a lot of money for something that looks entirely custom and professional.

MailChimp-compatible templates are not that expensive (though I do recommend a passing knowledge of html—not programmer level, but tweaker level). MailChimp offers free, simple integrated designs that require NO html as well—they're drag and drop and super user-friendly. It doesn't take much effort to make a nice-looking newsletter.

CONTENT IS KING

Find a balance between your own news and general news your readers will find interesting. Most authors don't want to shine the spotlight too heavily on themselves, but the reader *did* sign up for *your* newsletter, so they obviously want to hear your news. Temper your content with a mix of you-focused news and other topics that are relevant to your readers, either in terms of subject, genre, other books, etc.

In my own newsletter, I start with three articles about me and my books, then follow that with three articles that I've found interesting that I believe my readers would enjoy. Topics range from NASA missions to robotics to research on the brain, but they're topics that readers who like my type of books will also want to read.

To gather the news articles, I gather links together that I find interesting throughout the month. Sometimes I use a Chrome add-on called OneTab, sometimes I just email myself links to cool articles, videos, or other things I want to include. Then, at the end of the month, I just compile the links into the newsletter. Super easy.

SUBJECT LINES

Make a new subject line for each newsletter that's designed similar to click bait. "Click for a free coupon to my latest book!" is a successful subject line I've used, as is, "Exclusive cover reveal inside!" When I don't have major book news, I rely on my articles to develop a headline, such as "Art, Astronomy, and the Best Astronaut Photograph Ever." Aren't those subject lines more likely to make a reader open the email than "Beth Revis's Monthly Newsletter?"

Also consider five-touch marketing, and know that the subject line may be the reader's only touch they get from you. Not everyone is going to bother clicking to open the email, but they will likely at least look at the subject line—so make it something that will remind them of you and your work.

EXCLUSIVE CONTENT

I consider my subscribers to be my hardcore fans. They want to know about my stuff enough that they signed up for it to be in their inboxes. Therefore, I try to make the content worth their while. I held back my cover reveal so they'd be the first to see it. When my new book comes out, they get a coupon for a discounted copy. Not every newsletter has to be as big as a cover reveal—but I try to come up with something that real fans of the books would like each month. One month, it could be five fun facts about developing the story, the month before that it could be fun places I go to find inspiration. But there's something special there for my readers every time.

AUTORESPONDERS

Sometimes called "automation," an autoresponder is an email sent immediately (or scheduled) to people who subscribe to your newsletter for the first time. You could offer a free short story, a coupon for an ebook, some exclusive information, etc. This is a great way to keep readers engaged and entice them to sign up in the first place.

If you don't have anything to say other than, "thanks!" this may not be the best option for you. Don't clutter inboxes unless you have something of value to add. Most subscription services will automatically give new subscribers a thank you confirmation regardless, so there's no point in just saying thanks without offering something additional.

OPEN & CLICK RATES

The open rate is the number of people who actually opened up your newsletter and read it. The click rate is the number of people who clicked on a link in your newsletter.

Keep an eye on these rates when you switch things up to make sure that readers like the change, but don't obsess. For one thing, they're notoriously inaccurate—readers who use preview programs on their emails are likely not going to be recorded. Keep in mind also that as your subscribers go up, your statistics tend to go down. This isn't a bad thing; it's natural. If you have a hundred subscribers, and 75% open the email, you have seventy-five people who read your newsletter. But if you have a thousand subscribers and only 50% open the email, you have five hundred readers—a far better number, even if it's a lower percentage. Also remember that your early subscribers are probably going to be the hardcore fans who adore you (including your mom and your spouse), so of course they're more likely to open anything from you. But the more subscribers you get, the more casual fans you get—and that's good. Your reach is widening and your reader base is growing. They may not open every email, but they still like you and what you have to say.

Teacher's Guides

A TEACHER'S GUIDE IS A downloadable or printed handout for teachers to use to lead classroom discussions on their works. This is particularly helpful if your book has a high appeal for teachers—such as middle grade books, YA books dealing with topics that are a part of the high school curriculum, nonfiction books that students can use, and so on.

Some publishers will invest in a teacher's guide for a book, especially if it has a large school and library market. You could also pay a specialist to write a teacher's guide for you. However, if you want to tackle it yourself, it's not that hard.

BASICS OF A TEACHER'S GUIDE

Cover page: It's helpful to include the book cover, title, and even a brief synopsis on the first page of your guide. Sometimes, teachers will download several guides at once; don't make it hard to identify yours. Likewise, include a header or footer on every page with your name, the book title, and the page number of the guide. Remember, these guides will likely be printed and passed around. It's also helpful to include, somewhere, a link to your book.

Activities: You can develop pre-reading, during reading, and/or post-reading activities. Use a variety of activities. Most teachers will want something that's writing based, but also include activities that use charts, interactive media, history, art, drama or public speaking, and other skill sets.

• For pre-reading, consider opinion or imagination-based activities, such as hypothetical questions. If you're writing a futuristic world, ask students to draw a picture of a futuristic city. If your character faces some tough decisions early on in the book, have students write what they would do in a similar position.

• During-reading activities could include illustrations of the characters, guesses of what will happen in the end, research on historical or literary inspirations and allusions, etc.

• Post-reading activities could include reflection essays, rewriting of the end or speculating on what happens next, writing more about background characters, writing from the villain's point of view, illustrating a scene or characters, research projects based on topics in the book, etc.

• Discussion questions: Some guides have chapter-by-chapter questions; some are reserved only for the end or at the end of specific sections. Discussion questions are one of the most valuable resources of a teacher's guide, and some guides *only* have discussion questions. Look for questions that would inspire debate and conflicting opinions—yes or no questions or questions based on facts aren't as strong. Ten strong questions are better than a hundred weak ones— remember, you're not writing a test for students; you're inspiring dialogue.

• Vocabulary: More common for middle grade guides than for YA books, a list of potential vocabulary words can be helpful. Shoot for either 5-10 per chapter, or 25 or so total for the book, depending on the style of guide you're writing.

GENERAL TIPS

Remember that most of these guides will be printed, and if you design an actual worksheet, they'll be copied. Therefore, limit the graphic design of your guides. As a teacher, I expected the first page to be full of color and design—and I never printed that page. If the entire guide took a lot of ink to print, I typically didn't bother. Be aware of your user's needs.

If you can, link your activities and questions to the school curriculum. These guidelines may change soon, though, but standards are always available to the public online. The current guidelines can easily be found by a simple Google search for "Common Core ELA high school," which will bring you a list of the curriculum for most American high schools in English/Language Arts. It's simple to scan the list, pull out the Common Core numbers that fit your activities, and list them with your guide. It takes a few extra minutes on your part, but makes the guides incredibly more valuable for teachers, most of whom are required to have the Common Core standards for their lesson plans.

Don't limit yourself to novels—in fact, if you have short stories or novellas available, many times they're *more* valuable to a teacher than a whole novel. Teachers can only teach so many novels per year, and the ones they have access to depend on their school's budgets. Short stories and novellas, on the other hand, are much easier to access for teachers to share with students. If you have a free short story, include the story with the teacher's guide—and with a short bibliography of your other works so interested students can find you.

Swag

"SWAG" IS THE COMMON TERM for print marketing materials, most commonly bookmarks. Here are some simple items to include in your swag and advice on using them, but don't be afraid to think outside the box. Always keep in mind the costs and and pay-off of all swag.

When determining what kind of swag you want for your book, think of how you're going to use it. If you're going to mail it to people, get something flat that can fit in an envelope. If you're going on the road with your books, something a little bigger, such as pin buttons, may be a great way to attract readers to bookstores. Likewise, holding a few contests with some unique swag can help you stand out.

A major purpose of swag is branding. Your book's cover is your best brand, so don't make swag until you have a final book cover—and I mean *final*. Book covers can change, even after they're "done" (particularly if a major retailer thinks it won't sell well). Just because a cover is on an ARC doesn't mean it's final. Be in touch with your publisher about any changes in the book cover before you spend money and time on swag.

If you have a little skill in graphic design, it's not hard to make the basics of swag. It's also not hard to find qualified people who can design things for your book if you'd rather go that route.

And, as usual, keep in mind that your mileage may vary. I'm listing here things I've used or seen used, and often giving an opinion on their effectiveness. Ask another author, and you may get a totally different response.

BOOKMARKS

Your book cover should be somewhere on the bookmark. You could highlight a certain element of the book's cover (such as a cool title treatment or an evocative background) instead of the whole cover, but it should fit with the brand of your cover.

Other things to include or consider:

• **A tagline or brief description**. Go for short. People don't want a full book summary on a bookmark. If there's not room for this, you don't need it.

• **ISBN number.** Libraries and school systems are great places to leave your bookmark. They're also the ones most likely to use an ISBN number to look it up.

• **Publisher name and/or logo.** The sad truth? Some people judge the quality of a book based on whether it's self published or not. If you're traditionally published, put your publisher on the bookmark to show that you have a publisher—and make sure the house name is included, not just the imprint. If your book is self published, don't put anything down, even if you have a publisher name for your company.

• **Website for more info.** You can probably include something like social media links, etc., but at the very least, have a website to direct people who want more information. If you use a QR code, consider having a static link in text as well.

• **Room to sign.** People who can't afford your book will want a bookmark that they can then refer to and buy it later—having a spot to sign the bookmark makes it that much more valuable. *Note:* unless you're okay using a Sharpie all the time, consider getting matte instead of glossy, at least on one side, so that you can sign more easily.

• **Style.** Typically, I think the front of the bookmark is for art and to look eye-catching, and the back of the bookmark is for information.

• **Simple is better.** Most people try to cram everything they can onto a bookmark, but that tends to look unprofessional. You're not putting the whole book on the bookmark; it's just a teaser, and more influenced by the graphics and design than by the words. People want to glance at it, not study it.

Size: There are several typical size of bookmarks, but whether you go for wide or thin or medium, make sure it'll fit in a standard business-sized envelope for easier mailing purposes. You can also fancy a bookmark up by making it thicker than normal, but avoid going too thick—that can damage a book and not be the kind of thing the average reader wants.

How many should you get? I have a lot of various swag leftover, but one thing that always goes, and goes fast, is bookmarks. Most print shops will place orders in units of five-hundred or a thousand. I typically get batches of one to two thousand bookmarks, and rarely have trouble with that. However, keep in mind that book covers change, most often between hardcover and paperback, and that if you're writing a series, you'll want to update with new information. Therefore, you'll likely want to start with fewer bookmarks and replenish stocks after covers become more certain and permanent and after you get more information on the series's next releases.

If your book is an e-release only, you should consider a postcard instead of a bookmark.

Note: if you're carrying stacks of heavy, glossy paper (such as bookmarks or postcards) in a carryon for a flight, separate them into smaller bundles to avoid being inspected by TSA.

POSTCARDS

Postcards are my secret weapon. I never realized how beneficial they were until I started using them, and I see them often ignored by writers.

More than just for mailing: Yes, you can mail postcards. But you can do a lot more than that. Use them as notecards and include them when you mail a prize to a reader. Slip them into books when you do stock signings—they have more room for information than a bookmark. Take them with you to school and library visits—there's lots more room to sign and personalize for students and other people who may not be able to buy your book right away.

Design elements: A postcard size lends itself to a book cover size—it's easy to just make the cover of the book be the front of the postcard. But you can also be a little more graphic here, including a neat way to show off all the books in a series, or something else. Bookmarks are fairly standard, but you have the chance to do something far more unique for a postcard.

The front of a card should be very attention-getting and in color, perhaps glossy. But what you intend to do with the bookmark may dictate the back. If you never plan to mail the cards out, spring for more design and color. If there's a chance you'll mail them out, go for matte and black and white (a cheaper option that also allows you to write on them). Just because they're black and white doesn't mean you can't use design elements, such as a logo or fancy text for a tagline.

Somewhere on the card, probably the back, consider having:

• ISBN number

• Publisher name/logo

• Website/QR code

• Return address, if you're planning on mailing at least a portion of the cards

• Space to sign, plus space to add a mailing label (if that's an option), and/or space for a brief note

Size: Large postcards certainly stand out…but they're also a pain in the butt to mail. If you're using these cards primarily to supplement bookmarks at live events, go big. But if you're planning on using the cards more universally, consider a four-by-six inch option that will fit in a standard envelope—or even an odd-size card that's specifically shaped to fill the standard envelope.

How many should you get? If you're planning to do a mass mailing with postcards, get at least fifty more than you think you need—you'll use them, and it's good to have backups. Typically, I get about half the number of postcards that I get of bookmarks. Bookmarks go quicker (and often in sets of 20+ for libraries and classrooms), so getting about half that number for postcards has worked well for me. I also tend to get just bookmarks for the first book, and wait I have book covers for the entire series before getting postcards.

BUSINESS CARDS

I have never really found business cards helpful. If you want, you can get some printed up with basic information that you can distribute at, for example, a librarian convention when you want to offer them to contact you for a school visit, but in general, a bookmark is a very effective business card for a writer, and a website has all the information you'd typically be willing to give out to people.

While a traditional business card hasn't been much help for me, you can still do creative things with cards. If you have character illustrations, make profile cards for each of them. Print accolades on the card to slip into the book during stock signings to showcase its awards. If you have an evocative quote or tagline, you could use a business card as a mini art print.

OTHER FLAT PRINTED ITEMS

When you're mailing swag, flat items rule. Look at the options at your print shop, and you may figure out fun things to do with standard print shop materials. Here are some examples, but be creative!

Art cards: I use a postcard print service to make art cards. I commission a work of art directly related to my books, and I get permission from the artist to use the art on the cards first. Then I use a standard postcard sized print run to make the art cards, using full color and gloss on both sides. They don't look like postcards, but that's all they are—which makes the costs far reduced.

Stickers & Magnets: Business people will often have their business cards reprinted on same-sized magnets and stickers—a common enough practice that these sizes are standard at many print shops. They're also flat, easy to mail, and fairly cheap...and sized almost perfectly for a book cover. Rather than make an actual business card, put your book cover on the front, or design a unique sticker/magnet that goes with your book, just restricting it to the dimensions of a business card so you can print it cheaper.

Recreations of book items: If your book's characters use a flat print item, recreate it. I've seen historical romances create dance cards or calling cards for their characters using postcards or business card print services. I've even see a murder mystery writer use standard tag labels to create faux toe tags. Does your character use playing cards or tarot cards? A book with an evocative setting may get a "Wish you were here" postcard from that setting. These are all unique, easy to make and ship items that fans will love—but a word of caution. Make sure somewhere on the item is information about you and your book. I think a good balance is to have the front be the recreation of the item, but the back be a standard advertisement for your book. You want someone who's not heard of your work before to be intrigued enough to pick up the swag (from the front image) but informed enough to buy the book (from the back information).

Mini books: I shamelessly stole this idea from several different romance writers after carefully examining the swag in my RT Booklovers Convention Registration Bag. The idea is to use a "folded business card" available at most print shops—it's almost like two business cards hinged together on the long side. Several authors will put their book cover on one side, open the card up to a small sample chapter or description on the inside, and buy information on the back. I altered this, so that the front showed all three covers of my trilogy, the inside showed blurbs and accolades, and the back had links and information. I made mine so that they can stand up on a table like a little tent, displaying the covers, rather than open up like a book, but both are unique, fun ideas. Alternatively, many people will use regular business cards to show the book cover on one side, and a short description or teaser on the other.

Tear away tickets: When I wanted to build my newsletter list, I made tear away tickets custom printed with book art. These tickets are typically used to admit people into an event—they're perforated on one side so that the vendor can keep one side of ticket and the attendee can keep the other side. I used them to have a book advertisement on one side (which the reader keeps) and a place for the reader to put her name and email address on the other—which she drops into a bucket at a signing, after which I draw a winner for a prize. The readers get a unique piece of professional looking swag to keep, I get addresses for my newsletter and an easy way to draw for a prize.

BOOKPLATES

The purpose of a bookplate is for you to sign something that a reader can put in her own book when she can't meet the author in person. They're typically mailed to readers who can't attend a live event, but they're also very popular among students at classroom visits who may not have the means to immediately purchase a book.

There are a lot of services that design and print bookplates, but these tend to be used so rarely that it's not worth the cost—particularly when you design them to match one book, but then have subsequent book releases that also need bookplates.

I've used business card stickers before—a simple design with just my website printed on them—but the disadvantage to this is that most of the business card stickers are default glossy, not matte. In the case of bookplates, matte is far better than glossy—even if you don't mind using a Sharpie, the dry time for them can be excruciating, particularly if you have to sign dozens at a time for a mass mailing.

A nice compromise—especially if you're still waiting to see if you'll actually be using bookplates—is to get just plain white labels from an office supply store. You can jazz them up with a sticker or stamp—but in reality, someone asking for a bookplate is just asking for your signature, so you don't have to go too crazy over this one.

STICKERS & MAGNETS

These items are often very popular among younger readers—typically magnets can go in student lockers and stickers can go anywhere. They're also flat and easy to mail, but can get expensive, so price compare. Don't forget to add a website at the bottom in small letters so people who see the sticker/magnet out in the world can know where to go for more information.

Note: a huge stack of magnets in a carry-on are almost certain to get your bag inspected by TSA, so go ahead and take them out of your bag if you're boarding a flight.

TEMPORARY TATTOOS

Some people have had great success with temporary tattoos, particularly when they're linked to the book, but keep in mind that they're *temporary*—they'll be effective to advertise the book to the person who uses them and a few others, and then they're gone. On the flip side, a poster hanging in a classroom, a magnet in a locker, or a stack of bookmarks in a library have a greater reach.

Keep in mind also that skin tones change the look of the image, and writing can be hard to read, which may make a temporary tattoo of your book cover indiscernible.

When I was a teacher, an author agreed to do a Skype visit and provided the whole class with bookmarks and temporary tattoos. The tattoos were a huge hit—the kids had them plastered all over their skin. But the next day (when the tattoos were washed off), I asked the kids what they thought about meeting the author, and more than half of them didn't even remember her name, much less her book title.

If you're at a specific event looking to build buzz, though, temporary tattoos can be very effective. Imagine a crowded book festival where all the kids are wearing your temporary tattoo and pointing back to your booth to let others know where they got them. Be selective in the design and how you hand out temporary tattoos and they can be very innovative.

PIN BUTTONS

Pin buttons are hugely popular, particularly among teens, and are snatched up at signings like candy. They can also create buzz—when the teen puts it on her book bag, for example, they can tell others about your book.

The disadvantage to pin buttons are that they're hard to mail—they fit in an envelope, but they often get destroyed in the mail if they're not protected by extra padding. But they're an awesome thing to display at live events, and they're fairly inexpensive.

RUBBER BRACELETS

Bracelets—similar to the yellow Live Strong bracelets—are popular for swag. An advantage is that they're far easier to mail than pin buttons—they squish down and pop right back in shape. The disadvantage is that their effectiveness is hit or miss. They're often hard to read from a distance, and not as visually enticing as pin buttons. On the other hand, they tend to last longer and can be great conversation starters.

POSTERS

Posters—typically of just the book cover, but sometimes more graphically designed—are often great resources. Take them to signings (and sign them) for readers. Mail them to schools and libraries. Use them as part of a bigger prize.

The big problem with posters is that they're hard to ship. Play around with size on this. You can get posters that are prefolded to the size of a sheet of paper, making it easy for them to fit in most mailers.

T-SHIRTS

If you have a specific plan to use the t-shirts, they can be highly effective. Consider my advice on temporary tattoos—coordinating an event where a large number of people are showcasing your work is a great idea to spread the word.

However, t-shirts are expensive to make and ship (especially in low quantities), and they have the added worry of getting the right size for the right reader. Whenever a piece of swag has complications and expense, don't invest until you have a specific plan for them.

JEWELRY

I've used jewelry in the past . . . until a reader offered to give me back the (rather expensive) piece of jewelry. She'd only entered my contest for a bracelet and signed books to get the books. A piece of jewelry can be a great way to gain some notice for your book, but like t-shirts, they're inherently limited in their effectiveness. Some people won't want jewelry at all; some won't prefer the type you send. If your book has a specific piece of jewelry that applies directly to the book, it may be neat to have it made, but consider whether it's more worthwhile to work with a seller to provide the jewelry for sale or whether it's better to create a few custom pieces to give away for readers.

COSTS

When it comes to costs, you're really looking to spend pennies on the dollar per item—including shipping costs, if you plan to mail. Choose which items of swag—*if any*—you feel can help you sell books. Later in this section, we'll talk about gifts to readers, but swag's main purpose is selling books. You make an investment in purchasing the swag and hope it pays off in purchases of your book.

I *love* swag...but it's very easy to overbuy these items. If you're investing more than a dollar per item of swag or per swag bundle you're sending readers, you're likely losing money. Think carefully about this; it's a business decision that you need to make with a business mindset.

Preorder Promotions

A PREORDER PROMOTION IS WHEN you offer a gift or other incentive to people if they purchase your book before its launch date.

INCENTIVE

In order to entice people to preorder your book, it's best to offer something unique and valuable to the reader.

Note that this value isn't monetary. You don't want to kill all your profits in doing this campaign. A special signed bookplate and swag works well, but so does access to an in-world short story, cut scenes, or character profiles online.

When I come up with incentives, I tap my inner fangirl. What would I, as someone who fangirls about a book, want as a gift for preordering the book? For me, it's about exclusivity—something special for fans of the book who go the extra mile. It doesn't have to expensive, just special.

EXCLUSIVE TO ONE STORE

You can focus on just one store during a preorder campaign. Anyone who purchases your book for preorder from a specific store would get the incentives; all other preorders do not.

Advantages: This will help develop a positive relationship with your local bookstore—you are funneling all your sales directly to them. Additionally, doing it through a local store will enable you to easily offer not just the prize incentive, but a signed book as well. Your focus will be tighter on the store, and you'll have greater access to promoting the event locally.

Disadvantages: You're excluding people who are purchasing your book elsewhere, and excluding other stores. Some people won't bother going the extra mile to purchase from a non-local store, thereby limiting your customer base.

EXCLUSIVE TO MULTIPLE SELECT STORES

Rather than working with just one store, you could work with multiple stores across the nation. Typically, people select independent bookstores for this type of promotion. Look at which stores have done similar promotions in the past and consider targeting them. Alternatively, you could target ones that are all within driving distance for you and thereby offer signed books with the promo, or you could design a mini-book launch tour and hold events in conjunction with the preorder campaign.

Advantages: You'll reach a wider customer base when you involve more stores. If you're angling to hit a sales list, select stores that report to the *NY Times* to host your preorder campaign (hint: look at the stores where publishers send their authors on book tours or where other preorder campaigns are hosted).

Disadvantages: Sometimes, preorder incentives get lost in the shuffle; bookstores are busy, and if you're not physically there to help out, they may not be able to push your campaign as much as you like. It's also more difficult to sign books at stores that are further out, and some readers won't be satisfied with bookplates.

OPEN TO ALL PREORDERS

You don't have to make the preorder promotion store-specific; you can offer an incentive for *all* preorders. If you do this, select an incentive that is easy to mail (something flat and that will fit in an envelope) because mailing costs count toward your total investment. Alternatively, you could offer a digital incentive, such as the password to a secret page on your website, a coupon code for an ebook, or a download of a short story.

Should you require proof of purchase? That's up to you. It's difficult to keep track of, and the added complication may limit who is willing to participate.

On the other hand, if your incentive is costly or limited, you may want to have proof.

Be sure to check with local laws on "free gift with purchase" policies.

Giveaways & Contests

I'M A HUGE FAN OF DOING GIVEAWAYS and contests—huge! They're a great way to reach a wider audience and at the same time give back to the audience you already have.

SET UP

Organization of entries: You can either design the contest yourself (i.e. anyone who comments or tweets is entered), or you can develop an online form to organize the entries for you. Both Google Forms and Rafflecopter are popular sources.

Goals: Your giveaway should be focused on a goal, and then entries should be geared to serve that goal. In general, the point of a giveaway is to gain exposure, either currently or in the future. If you want to gain exposure for something right now, have your entries be focused on entrants sharing the information you want exposure for. *Example*: people are entered for each time they share your book cover on various different forms of social media.

If your goal is to build up for future exposure, then your entries will be focused on gaining new subscribers and followers. *Example*: people are entered if they follow you on Tumblr. This may not seem like much a distinction, but it's the difference between having people enter by retweeting a message and exposing that message to their friends and having them enter by following you Twitter—and therefore being exposed to future messages you send to them.

Certainly you can do both for a giveaway—especially when it comes to Twitter, which is very simple. But having a clear goal will help you focus and develop a better giveaway designed to meet that goal.

Prizes: Remember your audience. The thing they want is *your words.* It's not about the monetary cost of the prize—you're not Oprah, passing out free cars to everyone in the audience. It's about giving your fans the thing they're a fan of. Much like the best swag is something that's exclusive to your book, the best prizes are too.

This is true for two reasons. The first is because a prize with a high monetary value *will* get you more entries . . . but those entries aren't good ones. Say you give away $100 cash, and to enter, someone follows you on Twitter. A lot of people will follow you . . . and then either unfollow or ignore you for the rest of time. These aren't quality entries. They're basically paid followers, and they're not invested in you and your work, they're invested in winning a prize. Giving away something in connection to your work ensures that the people who enter care about your work in the first place.

The second reason to focus prizes on book-relevant items is because it's just not worth it to do otherwise. A few years ago, giving away an ereader (such as a Kindle or Nook) was a popular prize. It's far less popular now because most people have a preference for their ereader. If they want one, they buy it—and they buy a specific one that suits their specific needs. Sure, the prize has a high monetary value, but it's not something that is universally desired by your audience, even if it's linked to reading.

Even if an ereader costs a lot of money, at the end of the day, it's still something a reader can potentially buy for herself. People don't care as much for a prize they could just purchase themselves; it's not special. If, instead, you offer something unique that's specifically tied to what they do want from you—words—you'll get a much better reception. This can be as simple as a signed book (unique because it has your signature; it's not something they can easily purchase with a few clicks of a button) or more complex, but make sure it's tailored to your audience and is a prize your audience would value in their own way.

Entry types: There are two things to consider when you develop ways for people to enter your giveaway: what your goal is and what the prize is. Knowing your goal will help you focus on what people need to do to enter. Knowing your prize will help you know how much you can reasonably ask of people.

It's super simple for a reader to follow you on social media or even to like or share content. Ask your readers to do more than click a few buttons, though, and you need to reward them with something bigger.

When I was first starting out, I was fascinated by fan art and really wanted to see more of it. I offered a prize to people who did fan art of any kind based on my books. Had I offered nothing but a single signed book, I don't think I would have gotten many entries; I was asking a lot of my readers, and I needed to give them something good in return. So the prize was a combination of signed books and exclusive swag and lots of things people couldn't get otherwise.

You shouldn't think of giveaways and contests as "I paid for this, so they should give me that." It doesn't work that way—you can't guarantee that your prize will be worth any entries, and you shouldn't look at prizes as payments.

Instead, it's healthier to approach giveaways as a way to give back to your readers. You're finding something awesome for them to have because they've treated you awesomely.

JOINT GIVEAWAYS

You can always do a giveaway or contest on your own, but don't forget the power there is in numbers. Team up with other authors who write books like yours and do a big prize—if ten authors each contribute one signed copy of each of their books, each author is only out a book, but the winner gets ten.

Advantages: Doing joint giveaways mean that you share the load of not just the prizes, but also the advertisement. Each author participating brings their own audience to the table, and everyone's reach grows exponentially. Readers who like my book may now discover yours and vice versa. Authors participating get a wider reach and a bigger prize to offer readers.

Disadvantages: You generally have little control over entries. Most successful joint giveaways are structured simply—such as, "Follow every author on Instagram and win." This means the contest is focused on one task on one platform, so if you're trying to boost your individual newsletter, for example, this won't help much. Additionally, there's less focus on you specifically. While you may be exposed to Author A's larger audience, there's a change that the audience won't cross over, or will instead latch on to Author B's works instead of yours.

If you do a joint giveaway, consider if this would be a good time to also do a solo one. You may want to put your book on sale or offer another incentive to entice readers to engage with your work on a deeper level than just garnering another entry.

Also, if you have one specific branch of social media you want to boost, consider organizing your own joint giveaway. If you want more Twitter followers, join up with more authors and see if they'd be willing to do a Twitter-focused joint giveaway.

HIDDEN COSTS

There are definitely some hidden costs in giveaways and contests that you should keep in mind as you organize your promotions.

Shipping is killer. When my shipping expenditures crossed over $500, I knew I had to get it under control. Keep a close eye on how much you've spent on shipping. Consider shipping costs of prizes, and let that influence which prizes you select. I hate folded posters, for example, but it costs pennies to ship a folded poster and dollars to ship a rolled-up poster in a shipping tube. International shipping is even more expensive. Some websites, such as Book Depository, offer international shipping for free; if you can't afford to ship a prize internationally, consider having an alternate prize if an international winner is selected, or limit a certain percentage of your prizes to your country only.

Lost sales due to heavy promo. If you have too many giveaways, you may actually be hurting your sales. You don't want the reader to get the impression that your book is valueless and is constantly being given away. You also don't want to flood your social media feeds with constant giveaways that turn your followers from readers who are seeking your content to users who are just seeking a prize.

Expensive prizes don't equal sales. At the end of the day, you need to consider if what you're spending on the prize is worth what you're getting in return. You are not going to see a one-to-one ratio of dollars invested in prizes to dollars earned in book sales. Maintain a budget, and don't go overboard. Much like mothers appreciate handmade gifts, readers appreciate gifts designed for them much more than something that's attached to a lot of dollar signs.

Bonuses for Readers

YOUR BOOK IS ALL YOU OWE your readers. But as someone who is a part of fandom, I want to give back to my readers on a fan level, something more than just my book. This can be through swag or giveaways and contests, or simply through additions online or special bonuses for people who attend signings in person.

Additional Works: Cut scenes, short stories, flash fiction, and novellas are all great ways to give dedicated readers something extra. You can post them on your own website or in your newsletter, but consider open platforms, such as WattPad, which may be easier for the average reader to use and has the added advantage of potentially drawing in new readers.

Art: I love fan art, and I love seeing my characters and worlds come to life. Consider reaching out to artists and commissioning a piece of work for your book. You can (with permission and payment) use the work on printed materials, or you can (again, with permission and payment) upload it on your website. Try searching DeviantArt or Tumblr for artists who are already making fan art of your work or whose style is appealing to you.

And think beyond just visual art! I've seen authors commission songs to be recorded for readers, develop jewelry or scarves linked to the books, nail polish that matches the covers, and much more. Be creative—that's half the fun!

Stamps: I love the idea of having special stamps that are used when readers come see an author in person. It adds a little extra touch to the signing, and encourages readers to make the extra effort to attend a signing. You can find a stamp that's already pre-made with an image or words that suit your book, or you can order custom stamps. You can print just the title of your book, or a tagline, website address, or anything else. They're surprisingly not that expensive—you can easily alter an address stamp into something custom for your book.

Advertisements & Sales

You have to spend money to make money.
Right?

Paying for Promotion

IF YOU'RE SELF PUBLISHING, you'll probably do some form of paid promotion for your book. If you're traditionally publishing, you may not have to do anything—but if your publisher support is flagging, consider paid promotional opportunities. Keep in mind that many paid promotional opportunities work better for self publishing specifically because the self publisher has the control of varying the price of her novel. That said, you may want to research options and approach your agent and publisher with the idea of a timely sale to coincide with more promo.

Remember: As with all promotional efforts, there are no guarantees. You can spend a hundred dollars and get ten thousand sales; you can spend ten thousand dollars and get none. Be smart. Don't trust people who promise to make you tons of money. If it sounds too good to be true, it is.

A lot of promo involves payment, from the obvious price tag of swag, to the cost of time in organizing a blog tour, to the cost of time and money in travelling to events. This section is about paying for advertisements, and you'll notice that this section is the shortest in the book. When it comes to effective advertising, there is no golden ticket. You have to have knowledge, luck, money, and time to make paid advertisements work . . . and even then, they might not.

HIRING A PUBLICIST

A publicist is basically someone who offers publicity—which is *not* the same as a marketing specialist. A publicist may line up interviews and articles in various forms of media and arrange live events. You can hire them for a specific project, such as for a book tour, or for a specific time, such as launch week.

If you're traditionally published, you should have a publicist in-house assigned to you. If you still feel that you need to hire a publicist, make sure to work with your in-house publicist to coordinate efforts. First, discuss whether or not it's worth your money with your agent, who has a better idea of what you can expect in-house.

If you're self publishing, discuss up front with the person you're thinking of hiring what your goals and expectations are. Many of the benefits of a publicist—such as getting high-profile interviews and features—are closed to self publishers, whether or not they have a publicist. You both need to have reasonable expectations of what publicity is possible for your book.

Keep in mind that some genres work better with a publicist than others.

HIRING A MARKETING PROFESSIONAL

I look at a publicist as someone who's selling *you*; a marketer is someone who's selling your *book*.

You can hire marketing a la carte, such as someone to make your website, someone else to make your bookmarks, etc., but if you're going for a very targeted campaign, you may want to work with one specific company that can brand your work across several platforms and give you advice on how best to get the marketing materials to your targeted audience. *Example:* a marketing specialist who arranges a blog tour, develops graphics to use across social media, and arranges prizes for giveaways during launch week.

PAID PROMOS

Promotional opportunities that are available to the independent author (either one who has self published or who is investing her own money in promotion) are often limited. Nevertheless, they *are* there...with varying levels of success.

Social media ads: These are the ads that are displayed on the sidebars or as promoted posts on social media. Facebook and GoodReads are popular places for authors to promote their work in this way.

Website ads: Some websites offer banner or sidebar advertisements on their sites. These include book-specific sites, some book reviewer sites, and more. If you choose to go this route, consider which sites you, as a reader, tend to go to for book information.

Paid features on websites: Some websites offer to feature your book—for a price. Before signing a check, ask for detailed information on how many visitors come to the site a day, what the click through rate is, what the average rate of return is, and any other relevant details.

Social media posts based on payment: Some groups—particularly on Facebook and Twitter—cultivate a following of readers, and offer to feature your books on their social media for a price. Before agreeing to this, make sure that the followers are legitimate followers, and not paid followers that will never actually see your post.

Newsletter Services: A growing marketing opportunity is to have your work included in a newsletter. Readers sign up for the newsletter, typically based on either a genre preference and/or a deal preference. Then the newsletter sends out a scheduled post to the subscribers about the book. For example, subscribers may be interested in romance and subscribe to a newsletter about new and upcoming romance novels, or a reader may just want the best deals and will subscribe to a newsletter that alerts them when books go on sale. The current leader in this market is BookBub—and it's such a leader that I have a whole chapter dedicated to it. However, other markets in this area are growing.

Purchasing Ads

WHEN IT COMES TO PURCHASING ADS, you need at least two of the following: a huge amount of luck, a huge amount of research, or a huge amount of cash. It helps to have all three.

Paid ads work for people with big budgets. And I mean *big*. This is why paid ads work for the giant publishing houses, but not so much for the average self publisher. Paid ads needs the big budget because they're a scattershot. You're exposing your ad to a hundred thousand people and hoping that it's relevant to a hundred.

With the right research, you can focus your paid ads a little more tightly, exposing the advertisement to exactly your audience. But this requires careful analysis of who your audience actually is, where they are hanging out in real life or online, when the best time to reach them, what format advertisement is most efficient, and much more.

And even if you have the budget and the research, you still need luck. You're hoping to find the right audience at the right time with the right advertisement; you're essentially trying to predict the behavior of strangers, and influence those strangers into parting with their cash for a book they may never have heard of.

It's definitely no easy task.

PAID ADVERTISEMENTS ON SOCIAL MEDIA

Most social media offers some form of paid content that you can participate in.

Approach cautiously.

Sometimes, the investment seems small. $20 will extend the reach of a post you make on Facebook, for example. But just having your post flash through someone's newsfeed may not be enough. Remember the rule of five touches? You've paid for one . . . they still need four more before they complete a purchase.

Social media ads can quickly go out of budget. A smaller-than-thumbnail advertisement may be all you can afford, but even if you pay for it, will anyone notice it next to the much larger, much flashier—and much more expensive—ad right next to it?

When you purchase ads, you're competing against the Big Dogs who have advertising professionals to launch a campaign and budgets to match. $20 for a boosted post or $50 for a tiny sidebar advertisement won't really do much, if anything at all. It may feel like a significant chunk of your marketing budget, but it's a drop in the bucket to organizations who have thousands at their disposal.

If you can afford to take a total loss on it, try investing a small amount and seeing if it benefits you. But if your marketing budget is tiny and you can't afford the loss, it's probably not worthwhile to spend your money in this way.

ADVERTISEMENT SITES

An advertisement site is a website dedicated to showing advertisements, typically the top deals on books. Sometimes, the sites use social media, such as a Facebook group geared posting links to book sales. It's almost never worth your time to pay for these advertisement sites. The investment can be small—many sites operate on a $5 model—but likewise your return is small, if anything. Here are some warning signs to consider:

Is the site aimed at readers or authors? If the site is aimed at authors—and how authors can purchase advertisements—how do they expect to reach readers, the ones they should be reaching to make those advertisements worthwhile?

Will the site share detailed analyses of the advertisement? A lot of Facebook and Twitter pages offer paid group posts—you pay the page the feature your book on their social media. On the outside, this looks great; the page has tens or even hundreds of thousands of likes. You're reaching a huge audience! Except . . . there's every chance that the audience was bought and therefore aren't readers and aren't engaged in the post at all. Additionally, unless the post is boosted (which costs more money) it's highly unlikely that even a small fraction of that audience will even see the post.

Are most of the followers of the advertisement site also authors? You don't want to be speaking to vacuum. If the advertisement site has a strong social media presence, scan who the followers are. Are they mostly authors? Many authors will follow a site they've paid to be advertised on, but they're looking out for their own books, not yours, and they're seeking justification of their investment. It's not worth your time to be shouting at someone to buy your book when all they're doing is shouting at you to buy theirs.

Is the site genre-specific? If so, does it focus on your genre? A site may be hugely qualified and totally legit, but if they mostly advertise paranormal romance and you've written a literary tragedy, you're not doing yourself any favors. Many sites will turn down a book that doesn't suit their audience, but some won't, and others may not be able to vet all ads. The onus is on you to make sure that not only is the site legitimate, but also that it will reach the kind of audience that's best suited for your work.

BookBub

AS OF THIS BOOK'S WRITING, the best investment of a writer's advertisement budget is with BookBub.

BookBub is a newsletter-based site. Readers enter their email address and the types of books they like, and BookBub alerts them of deals for those books.

BookBub can be expensive—depending on the genre, you could be spending several hundred dollars for an advertisement there. And to qualify, your book must be on sale, which means you'll be earning even less than you would on a normal sale. Regardless, BookBub provides an excellent chance on not only earning back your investment, but of seeing a huge spike in sales and profits. Many authors see success not just for their title on sale, but for all their titles as new readers tackle their backlist.

I obviously cannot guarantee this will happen, and I do know of some authors who've not earned back their investment. But if you're looking for a site to invest marketing budget in, BookBub is an excellent one to start with, and many authors feel it's the only one worth bothering with.

TIPS FOR GETTING A BOOK BUB AD

Traditionally published authors need to work with their publisher on getting a BookBub ad because the book has to go on sale, and the publisher sets the sale price. Additionally, the publisher may be able to expand a sale price reach by using outlets such as the Kindle Daily Deal, BN Buzz Books, and more. If you have a traditionally published book, discuss with your agent and publisher a plan to maximize a book sale . . . but be aware that just because you want to put your book on sale doesn't mean your publisher will do it. They set the price, not you.

Self published authors can set their own book price, and it's therefore easier for them to apply directly to BookBub for a spot. BookBub ads are notoriously difficult to get, however. They have very high standards—which is good for their readers, and ultimately good for you. BookBub is successful *because* of those high standards.

Be Professional: A slapped together book won't cut it. BookBub is one of the big dogs, so if you want a spot, you need a cover that's well done, an interior design that's well put together, and an edited book that has no errors.

Have Reviews: It's a total catch-22, isn't it? You need an ad to get reviews; you need reviews to get an ad. But BookBub wants some assurance of quality on the books they feature, so don't be surprised if a book with low reviews is rejected. There's no specific threshold, though, and there are other ways for BookBub to determine a book's quality, so even without reviews, you still have a shot.

Have a Sale Price: You not only have to have your book on sale to qualify for BookBub, it needs to be a sale price that's unique and special. There are time limits from when your last book sale was to when it will qualify for BookBub advertised sale. In other words, you can't put your book on sale every month and expect to get a BookBub.

Make sure you follow the guidelines for submission precisely. BookBub is very clear on what they accept and don't, and their guidelines are so specific for a reason—it helps make their site a success and your sale a success. If you're rejected the first time, wait a bit, build reviews, ensure your book's professionalism, and apply again.

Sale Strategies for Self Published Authors

BECAUSE SELF PUBLISHED AUTHORS are more in control of their book's pricing and placement, there are strategies that they can use that a traditionally published author cannot.

STACKING PROMOTIONS

While BookBub remains the king of paid advertisements, there are several other smaller, legitimate sites, including Fussy Librarian and Riffle, for example. Research the ones that work best for your genre, and consider doing a bigger blast using multiple sites.

You can do this in two ways. The first is to get advertisements for your sale from multiple sites and post them all on one day. So, for example, on Monday, fifteen different sites post about your sale. This means even if someone misses it on one site, there's a good chance they'll see it on another.

The second method is to spread your promotions out on a schedule. You could post five promotions on Monday, five on Tuesday, and five on Wednesday. If you're trying to boost your sales rank—which will lead to more natural sales from people on the store site rather than ones coming directly from your ad—think about where best to place your highest sales. Likely, BookBub will give you the biggest spike in sales, so making it be on the last day of your campaign means you'll be starting on a higher note and give yourself an even higher spike in sales.

In other words, if you *just* did a BookBub and your sales rank was at a thousand, at the end of the day, you could be in the top 500. But if you stacked your promotions and did some ads prior to your big one, then on Day One your rank may rise to 900, and on Day Two your rank goes to 700 and on Day Three your rank shoots to the top fifty.

Obviously this isn't a guarantee, and you need to weigh whether it's worth it to not only research, but also apply to and potentially pay for the smaller sites to run your advertisement.

TAKE ADVANTAGE OF THE SEASON

It's hard to think like a corporation, but when it comes to selling books, it often helps to emulate big businesses.

Think about your favorite brands. How do they market to you? How can you do similar marketing for your book?

Every time Black Friday and Cyber Monday roll around, I'm inundated with emails and tweets and everything else from businesses I've used in the past. Everything's on sale and vying for your attention—and dollar. And while this may mean you get lost in some of the shuffle, it also means that your audience is in the mindset of "buy." So put your book on sale and let your audience know. Chances are, your books will be swept into their shopping carts along with everything else.

I currently have two books that have green covers—*Shades of Earth*, the third book in my Across the Universe trilogy, and *The Body Electric*. Last St. Patrick's Day, I made a quick graphic with a title that said, "Why wear green when you can read green?" and put the two covers on it, along with purchase information. It was my best sales day that quarter.

During Valentine's Day, many publishers and authors will hold romance-inspired giveaways or contests linking back to the romance in their books.

Consider when people give gifts and take advantage of it. During the end-of-the-year holidays, offer to send people a free signed bookplate if they purchase your book, or set up with a local indie bookstore to sell signed copies of your book.

You don't want to constantly shout about your books and selling them—that makes you no better than spam. But if there's a fun link between your book and something going on with the season or year, take advantage of it. The goal isn't to find an excuse to bring up your book at every opportunity; it's to find ways to bring up your book when there's already an opportunity at hand.

STAGE UPCOMING BOOKS WITH SALES

A loss leader book is one that you're willing to take a cut in profits on in order to maximize profits for another book.

You see this most often with series—Book One is typically the loss leader. When it launched, Book One cost $5.99. But by the time Book Three of the series is out, Book One costs $0.99, and the other books in the series still cost $5.99.

The reason for this is simple: The author wants to hook the reader with Book One so they offer it on sale, which leads to more sales of Books Two and Three.

You can use loss leaders for more than just a series, though. You can put a book on temporary sale (rather than permanently free—"permafree"—or always on sale) to celebrate the upcoming launch of a new book or new series. You can include sample chapters of a new series in an older book that's on sale, hopefully leading readers to invest in the new book. And you can use coupon codes to offer readers buy-one-get-one deals for new release titles.

Be creative and explore opportunities—think like a business!

Reviews & Events

There is nothing more exciting than
knowing someone else read
your work.

Selling Your First Book

YOU WROTE YOUR BOOK, you edited your book, you got a great cover for it, you formatted it in all the right ways, you listed it in the right categories (or your publisher did).

Now you want to sell it.

So, how do you, as a completely unknown debut author, sell your book?

. . . In a lot of ways, you don't.

This is a hard pill to swallow, and it's not an answer anyone wants to hear, but the truth of the matter is that there are a *lot* of books on sale out there, and your biggest problem is that you're one tiny voice in a cacophony of loud shouters.

Just publishing your first book isn't enough. No one will find it, and if they do find it, they won't invest in it. Think about the way you buy books, and how easy it is to put down a book from someone you've never heard of versus automatically buying a book from an author you love.

There is no secret to getting a big, splashy launch with tons of sales for your very first self published title. There is no secret because, frankly, it doesn't happen.

People can't buy your book if they don't know it exists, and even if they *do* know it exists, they *won't* tend to buy a book that has no validation—no reviews, no rank, no past books to prove the author's worth.

So: your goal as a debut author is to prove your worth.

It is not to have an epic launch. It is not to do a checklist of steps to ensure exposure. It's to prove your worth.

The First Step to Market Book 1: *Write Book 2.*

The biggest thing you can do in terms of developing a career as a author is to have more books available for people to buy. New books breathe life into old books, and they maintain your career. The more you good words you write, the stronger your career.

And if you self publish, having a long backlist means you're in a better position to put your first book on sale and use it as a loss-leader, encouraging people to take a chance on your writing. The more books you have, the easier it is to grow your audience, develop marketing plans, and encourage more sales.

The Second Step to Market Book 1: *Gather reviews.*

Traditionally published books have a mark of validity because, merely by going through the process of traditional publication, the book has been "approved by the gatekeepers," professionally edited, and there's a level of quality assurance from that vetting. In addition to that, it's easier for traditionally published books to garner reviews, not just from the big sites (like *Publisher's Weekly* and *Kirkus*), but also from bloggers and everyday people posting to retailer sites. Just because you're traditionally published, though, doesn't mean you'll get reviewed by the top sites, and you may have to do some legwork yourself to push for attention.

Self published books get that same vetting and validity that traditionally published books start with via reviews. The more reviews you have, the better—and not just glowing five stars, but legitimate, thought-out reviews, preferably on a retailer site such as Amazon. Think about the way you make purchases online (and most of your sales for a self published book will be online). You check out the reviews, right? So the way to get sales is to get reviews.

Of course, this won't happen overnight—which is why the big splashy debut of your first novel isn't likely to be big and splashy. Instead, you can build up your reviews over time, through using online review programs such as

NetGalley, hiring blog review tours, making connections on social media, using incentives in your newsletter, etc.

The Third Step to Market Book 1: *Find and cater to your readers.*

You're not going to get hundreds of followers overnight, and even when you have hundreds or thousands of followers, those numbers do not automatically equate sales. Therefore, don't, don't, don't fall into the trap of scammy followers, where you either pay for followers or do follow-for-follow campaigns. You want followers who actually care about you and your book, and an organically grown list may take far longer to develop, but will pay off in a far bigger way in the future.

But the most efficient way an author can market her book is by being in touch with her audience directly. Know your readers. Know what they want.

This doesn't mean you should pander to your audience. This doesn't mean you should write to the market. But it means you should *know* the market. You should analyze the books in your genre, think about why people love them. You should listen to your audience when they talk about the things they love in books—yours, and others'.

Learn. Never stop learning. And never stop trying to write a better book than the one you wrote before.

And honestly? That's about it in terms of effective marketing for your first book. Write the next book, garner reviews, build up your audience. There's really not that much else you can effectively do, and people who try to tell you otherwise are likely also trying to dig into your wallet.

This knowledge may certainly give you a sense of helplessness as you throw your beloved debut into the void. But remember: you're not in this for one book. You're in this for a career.

Gathering Reviews

ONE OF THE MOST IMPORTANT THINGS you're going to want as a writer is reviews.

Reviews mean someone has read your work. Reviews mean exposure and the chance for more people to read your work. They're the ultimate validation.

And they are really, really hard to come by, especially without a huge marketing push.

The first thing you need to know: There is no normal. This isn't like a growth chart for a baby—the number of reviews you get in the first month may be wildly different from the number your fellow authors get, and it means nothing, really. It doesn't mean one book is better than the other; it doesn't mean anything at all. There's no point looking up statistics on other authors who released their books around the same time as you. Their book isn't your book, and there's no normal for any set of books.

That said, reviews are important, and there are a few things you can do (and a few things you should never do) to help get more.

TO GET MORE REVIEWS

• *ARC Distribution:* Most publishers will print and mail out ARCs to readers, and many reviews will come from this distribution. If you're traditionally published, you'll have little say in how many ARCs are printed and sent out (or to where they're sent), but you can always ask for more if you have a plan on distributing some on your own. If you're self published, consider whether or not it's worth it to print ARCs of your book (typically either a proof copy or a finalized copy). Done in a targeted way, it may add a lot of incentive and value to the reader, but they are pricey.

• *eARC Distribution*: Many publishers use either NetGalley or Edelweiss to help distribute eARCs to readers. If you're self published, you can either sign up for NetGalley yourself (which is expensive) or join a co-op, typically on a monthly basis for a much smaller price. You can also contact reviewers individually and offer an eARC. Traditionally published authors—know that you should never send your manuscript for review electronically without your publisher's permission.

• *Blog review tour:* This is different from many blog tours because rather than you providing articles and interviews, each blogger participating in the tour offers to read and review your book, then post the review on a specific date during the tour. This can be a great way to gain exposure (and far more valuable than a typical blog tour). I suggest, however, *not* organizing this yourself; instead, go through a blog tour organization. As with all reviews, the more distance the author can give between herself and the review, the better.

• *Social Media:* Often, people just forget to review books. They like the book, but they don't review it. You could occasionally (maybe once every other month or so) mention on your social media how important reviews are to authors, and how a review can help make or break a book. Don't demand them, don't complain about not having enough—just remind people that they're important. You could also highlight reviews that have meant something to you, with the idea that one review begets another, but again, don't do this too often. You don't want to appear to be begging for reviews or bragging about current ones.

If you're self published, you can also add a small note in the back of your book reminding readers of the value of a review and that you appreciate their time in reviewing. Don't beg; just remind.

THINGS TO AVOID

• *Contests for reviews:* Although some authors have successfully leveraged contests for reviews, in general I advise to avoid this practice. You don't want people thinking that the only reason you have reviews is because you bribed people into leaving them. You don't want to be in a position where people are leaving false reviews in order to enter a contest. And you don't want to give the impression that you're only seeking out positive reviews.

    • *Spam for reviews:* If you are the type of person who sends mass messages to people on social media or GoodReads about leaving a review or cross-posting a review, please get off the internet. You clearly don't understand the difference between human interaction and spam. There is a difference between approaching an individual reviewer you think may like your book and spamming every single person who makes the mistake of following you on social media or adding you on GoodReads.

    • *Don't encourage family and friends to leave glowing reviews:* Come on, really? What are you, twelve? Sure, you'll get shiny reviews saying you're the next best thing, but they reek of inauthenticity. And more than that—there's a chance it'll get you kicked off Amazon and other sites, as this is a clear violation of their policies.

    • *Do not buy positive reviews:* Ever.

    • *Do not trade reviews:* Ever. This is when one author says, "I'll review your book if you review mine!" It's a pretty scummy thing to do, goes against most review sites terms of services, and can leave you in a terrible position. What if you hate the other author's book? Do you lie and rate it highly (because obviously the author expects a high rating)? Or are you honest—in which case, will the other author give you a poor rating in revenge? Doing this sort of thing is underhanded, egotistical, and forces you into awkward situations. Avoid at all costs.

    An important thing to remember: Negative reviews sell books.

    No, really.

    You *don't* want all positive reviews. You want all *honest* reviews. And an honest negative review will sell a book quicker than a false positive one. A false positive review is all sunshine and no depth. Many readers look straight to the negative reviews to get a real idea of whether or not a book is right for them. If the negative review says, "this book had a bittersweet ending, and I didn't like that," a reader who *does* like a bittersweet ending will snatch the book up.

Honest reviews—positive or negative—are the goal. Anything you do to create reviews that aren't honest, whether you use Grandma's account to give your book five stars or you pay someone else to do it, is a waste of time, a disservice to your readers, and underhanded. Don't be that type of person.

The Author's Role in a Review

YOU WROTE THE BOOK.

The reviewer read the book.

That is the end of your connection with the reviewer.

Don't argue with, comment, mock, obsesses over, or try to delete a review.

This seems like common logic, but enough authors have had issues with this in the past that it's worth mentioning.

Don't argue with, comment, mock, obsesses over, or try to delete a review.

Here's the thing when it comes to reviews: you are not a part of the process. Sure, you wrote the book. But once it's published, it's out of your hands. People will love it. People will hate it. People will give it five stars, or no stars, and it doesn't matter *because the book is written and published and out in the world and there's nothing you can do about the way people react to it.*

Yes, some people won't "get" what you were trying to do.

Yes, some people will get what you were trying to do and hate it.

Yes, some people will interpret your book in a vastly different way from what you intended.

Yes, some people are actually just trolls, seeking attention by being hyper-negative or comically incorrect.

It doesn't matter. The book is out there, you can't change it now, and the book is being judged based on one person's reaction to the text that's present.

Therefore: *Don't argue with, comment, mock, obsesses over, or try to delete a review.*

But the reviewer is *wrong!* She says X happens in the book, but it doesn't!

That sucks. Maybe she misinterpreted the book. Maybe she didn't read the book all the way through and made some assumptions. Let other readers correct the wrong review; they will.

Solution: Say nothing.

No, no—I mean the reviewer is *wrong!* She says that this thing about my book isn't realistic, but it's based on research and facts. She's factually incorrect.

Ignorance is bliss, isn't it? They think they're crusading for a truth, but they're wrong.

That blows. Sorry. But it's not your place to correct them. Post about your research and the facts on your own space, if you want. Most readers should be able to spot that the "fact" being spouted by the reviewer isn't correct, and even if they don't, there's a good chance they won't care.

Solution: Say nothing.

Okay, so, the review says something I wrote is terribly unbelievable, but it's based on something that actually, literally happened to me.

Truth is stranger than fiction. If you really want to set the record straight, don't write anything to the reviewer, just write about the real life experience that inspired that part of your novel on your blog or something. Don't correct or confront the reviewer directly.

Solution: Say nothing.

But the reviewer didn't even finish the book! She labeled it DNF (did not finish) and slammed me for what she had read—if she kept reading her problems would have been fixed.

Yeah, but she didn't keep reading. And a DNF review is valid—it lets other readers know at what point a reader gave up on a book. You can't make someone read your book if they didn't connect with it.

Solution: Say nothing.

But the reviewer wasn't professional *at all*. She used .gifs and was super sarcastic and mean!

Maybe you shouldn't read reviews. Reviews are where people give their honest reactions to books, and sometimes they like to do that in a comedic way.

Some reviews are professional, such as those by *Kirkus* or *Publisher's Weekly*. Some reviews, by readers on retail sites or review sites such as GoodReads, are not. They have different styles. Remember: they're talking about the *book*, not *you*.

Solution: Say nothing.

But the reviewer said I had bad grammar...and she has bad grammar in her review!

So? You wrote a book that was edited by professionals and you make a living using your words. The reviewer posted something online that was, at best, briefly scanned before posting. It's a different medium. You don't have to be an author to be a critic, and you also shouldn't judge a reader on the same level as a writer.

Solution: Say nothing.

But the reviewer is complaining about basic elements of my book, such as the fact that the teenage character is acting like a teenager.

Eh. It happens. Some people have different expectations of the genre. Some people just have personal pet peeves. You can't win 'em all. Sure, they're slamming you for something that's a basic, essential part of your genre. Maybe this is the first time they read that genre, and they're discovering it's not right for them. The very thing they hate may be something the next reader loves.

Solution: Say nothing.

But the reviewer just doesn't get what I was trying to do. If they read closer, they'd see the real point of the novel.

I remember reading a book about a boy who, in the beginning, is an utter jerk, but by the end of the novel, has learned his lesson and become a really great person. A lot of readers never got past the fact that the boy was a jerk—they couldn't shake the initial impression of him, but if they'd read with a more astute eye, they'd see the author was really showing a significant change of personality.

But you can't control the way people read. You can't control anything about the book/reader relationship. If they don't get it, they don't get it. It's not a failing of either you or the reader, it's a matter of taste.

Solution: Say nothing.

It's like the reviewer didn't even read the description. My book is *obviously* X, but they expected Y, and they hate it because of that!

Sorry, that sucks. It happens a lot with books that are "insta-buys," such as a book that's on a deep sale (they buy it for the price without really closely reading the description) or books that are very popular (they buy it because everyone else is reading it). But you wrote a sweet romance, and they expected a tragedy. Or you wrote a story with a fantasy twist, and they expected realism.

And they *hate* the book for it.

Don't worry about it. Negative reviews sell books just as much as positive ones. A reader who would rather have the element you wrote will love to know that it's there.

Solution: Say nothing.

But the reviewer rated my book…and it's not even *written* yet! That's not fair!

This happens most often on GoodReads, where readers can rate a book before it's even out.

They might do this for several reasons. Some people don't use the star system to rate books the way the system intends. Instead, a one-star may mean "most highly anticipated, the number one book to buy when it's available." It may mean the opposite. You don't know. People are using the star system for their own uses, and they have no obligation to explain it to you. And, frankly, sometimes people lie. They want to look important, so they pretend to have read a book that's not out yet. Don't worry about it. It doesn't happen often, and yeah, it makes your rates look low while you're still writing the book, but once it's out, that'll change quickly.

Solution: Say nothing.

The reviewer dinged my rating because of a personal pet peeve. She didn't like the character's name or the color of her hair or some other pointless detail. She completely ignored the story and just hated on this one minor thing.

Have you really never done that? I have. When I was a teacher, I knew this horrible person with a really unique name. If I see that name, I have a really hard time connecting to the main character. I just . . . can't see that name without remembering that person.

It's not fair. But it is reality. And if a reviewer just has a pet peeve that you happen to hit, it's really nothing to get too upset over.

Solution: Say nothing.

The reviewer *promised* to review my book. I mailed it out to her, and it took a lot of work to get it to her, and . . . nothing. (Or worse: after all that, I got a negative review!)

Sorry.

That's the way the game works. You can offer a book, they can accept the book, but they may not ever end up reading it. Some reviewers are greedy, and they just want a lot of ARCs. Some reviewers are swamped and overwhelmed—not just by reading, but sometimes real life interrupts the best-laid plans. Some reviewers have a policy to not give a poor rating and may choose not to rate your book at all in that case. Either way, the reviewer owes you no explanation, and they don't owe you a review. It may be, at worst, discourteous, but it's not like you made a contractual transaction. If you were under the impression that a review was forthcoming, you *may* want to contact the reviewer and just check and make sure she got the book, that it didn't get lost in the mail, etc., but either way: Suck it up and move on. If anything, you now know not to send that reviewer a copy of your book in the future.

Solution: Say nothing.

But the reviewer actually sent me a copy of her review. Of course I should comment then—she's asking for interaction!

Not necessarily. A lot of times, people will tweet you a review not because they want you to see it, but they forget that when they use a person's twitter handle, the person sees it—they're just trying to have a complete tweet. If someone tweets you a positive review, I, personally, don't see a problem with saying "Thanks!" But that's it. If it's negative, don't reply. If you don't want to see whether it's negative or positive, don't reply.

Some reviewers may go a step further, sending you emails of reviews that aren't glowing or are downright mean. Don't respond. There's a chance the person didn't realize that the review would offend you—seriously. I've written three-star reviews that I thought were really thoughtful and carefully written, but others thought they were mean and overly critical (one reason why I no longer write reviews). Maybe they did mean to bait you and get you to respond—so don't give them the satisfaction. *You don't have to respond to everyone who tries to communicate with you, especially if the communication is negative or a waste of your time.*

Solution: Say nothing.

But the reviewer is confusing me with the book. My character has someone who is evil/racist/sexist/cruel/whatever, but she's saying that I am that way. It's fiction!

Any reasonable reader will know there's a difference between the author and the characters. Don't argue with someone who can't see that. There's no point. Arguing with someone who's so off-base is a waste of your time.

Solution: Say nothing. Maybe also go get a drink.

But the reviewer is actually, literally making threats on me and/or personally attacking me. Not the book. Me.

This is the point where the reviewer has gone over the line. It's sad, regrettable, and rare, but sometimes readers cross the line to the point where they send threats to the author of the book, harass the author, or otherwise seek to actually harm the person of the author for whatever reason.

The same advice still applies. Don't comment or speak directly to the reviewer. If they've gone from reviewing a book to directly threatening your safety in some way—even if you don't think they'll actually follow through with the threat—you need to report this reviewer. Tell your agent and publisher. Report to the site where the review is published—don't just flag the review, but also send an email directly to the website, detailing why this review has crossed the line. If you feel your safety is in jeopardy, also contact your local police.

Don't turn this into a public debacle. If this is a serious threat, treat it seriously and go straight to the authorities.

Solution: Say nothing to the reviewer, but say lots of the authorities.

How to Respond to Negative Reviews

I HAVE A FRIEND WHO HATES PUPPIES. True story. She hates dogs, actually. One day, I asked her, "Okay, you hate dogs. I can kind of get that. Some people are scared of them, or were bit by one, or whatever. But what about puppies? Cute little wiggly puppies with waggly tails and puppy kisses."

"I hate puppies, too," she said.

Just like that. "I hate puppies, too."

I mean, COME ON.

I have a friend who hates Harry Potter. The whole franchise. There is not one thing she likes. She read part of the first book and put it down. She felt that the whole first half of the first book glorified child abuse. And yeah, I get her point. If you look at it that way, Harry is abused by the Dursleys, and honestly? They don't *really* get their pay back for the twelve years of abuse.

"But the book is about so much more than that," I told her, trying to get her to read on.

"Oh, I know—there's magic and Hogwarts and shizz," she said. "But I don't really care about that."

MAGIC AND HOGWARTS AND SHIZZ BUT I DON'T CARE ABOUT THAT.

My own husband hates chocolate. I didn't find this out until after we were married. That's the kind of thing that should be discussed, I KNOW, but it didn't even occur to me that anyone COULD hate chocolate. He's not allergic. I have a friend who's allergic to chocolate, and that's bad enough. But the husband? He just doesn't like it. And I'm *married* to this monster, y'all.

There are people in the world who hate bacon. Seriously. Not for any religious or ethical reason. *They just think it doesn't taste good.* There's a Facebook fan club that is just about hating bacon. There are 28 members (SO FAR) and they have BADGES. According to one online source, 11% of America's population HATES BACON.

There are what? 7 billion people in the world now? Statistically speaking, there has to be at least one person in the world who hates puppies, Harry Potter, chocolate, AND bacon.

My point? If there are people in the world who hate puppies, Harry Potter, chocolate, and/or bacon, then there are people in the world who hate your book. Put in that perspective, things aren't so bad, huh?

And if a negative review *really* gets you down? **Here's what to do: think about your absolute favorite book of all time.** We all have one. A book we *love*, one that's practically perfect in every way.

Got the book in mind? Now go to GoodReads. Look the book up. Filter the reviews for 1-stars (because I promise you, it *does* have one stars). And smile. Because if people can rate your favoritest book in the whole world with one star, then of course people can rate your book that way, too.

FUN FACTS

Harry Potter and the Prisoner of Azkaban (my fave of the series) has 5,556 one-star reviews at the time of this book's publication.

A Wrinkle in Time, one of the best science fiction titles for teens and young people, has 13,585 one-star reviews.

The Hitchhiker's Guide to the Galaxy, which is funny and insightful and a classic, has 20,274 one-star reviews. *Twenty thousand, two hundred and seventy four.*

Hamlet, written by Shakespeare, arguably the most popular work by the most influential writer in the English language, has 8,617 one-star reviews. *King Lear*, my personal favorite Shakespearean play, has nearly 2,500 one-star reviews.

Okay, okay, okay. We can all agree that some of those above titles might have elements that some people don't like. But who can dislike a classic children's picture book? Let's say...*Where the Wild Things Are*. I'm not sure, but I'd wager that's the most popular children's book in America. And it has over 11,524 one-star reviews. More then *eleven thousand people* individually clicked on the one-star rating for a *children's book. Curious George?* Nearly 2,000 one-stars. *The Cat in the Hat?* Nearly 6,000.

If there are people who hate these books, there are people who hate yours. Go pet a puppy, eat some chocolate and/or bacon, and read your favorite book again. Things aren't so bad. People are just ~~weird~~ *different* is all.

Doing Solo Events

LOVE THEM OR HATE THEM, book events are important. They put you face-to-face with your reader, and for some readers, authors—*you*—are their rock stars.

When you do a solo event, where it's just you in front of an audience, it's natural to feel intimidated. It helps to go in with a plan.

PREPARE MATERIALS

Select which passages from your book—if any—you plan to read aloud at the event. If you do want to read, select a passage that's no more than three pages long, preferably one that's even shorter than that. Honestly. While everyone always suggests that an author do a "reading," no one ever really enjoys them. Very few authors have a dynamic voice that can make a reading entertaining. Think about the difference between listening to a student read a passage of Shakespeare in a high school English class and listening to an actor read that same passage.

So select something short, something that's not a spoiler, and something that's entertaining—and again, make sure it's *short*. It also needs to be short not just in length, but also in terms of presentation—if you have to spend ten minutes setting up the passage, it's not worth it for you or the readers in the audience.

If you have any other materials, make sure they're prepared well in advance. Go over the things you want to say ahead of time, and keep in mind that you'll likely talk faster than you did when you practiced, so err on the side of extra content.

PREPARE FORMAT

There are several different ways you can develop what you want to do at a solo event. Again, I highly recommend that your event *not* be *just* a reading. You don't have to put on a pony show, but it helps if you think about what will be most interesting and entertaining to your readers.

If you're doing a casual affair, having some snacks out and milling around the crowd may be all you need to do. Arm yourself with small talk and a smile, and plans on what to do if only a handful of people show up.

If you're looking for something more structured, as most authors do, don't be shy about making an agenda for the event. Likely the bookstore owner will give you some sort of introduction—feel free to give her material if she doesn't know you well. From there, decide how you want to present your book. Many readers will talk about their inspiration, discuss how the book developed, do a small reading, and then take questions.

You may want to consider an interview format. If a fellow author lives nearby or if you're on friendly terms with the bookstore, they can interview you. This may require more work for your partner, who needs to prepare questions, and it may be easier if you help develop them. But an interview format creates a discussion that provides less pressure for you to entertain, and could feel less formal for all involved.

I also like to turn solo events into a game with the audience. I have five trivia questions that I developed from each of my fiction books. The questions aren't spoilers, and you don't have to have read the books to answer. Some deal with geography (*The Body Electric* takes place in Malta; what two nations are closest to this Mediterranean island?). Some deal with Easter eggs I've hidden in the text (In *Across the Universe*, Amy is frozen in cryogenic chamber #42, a reference to the meaning of life, the universe, and everything in what famous sci fi novel?). I picked questions that I felt would appeal to a large variety of people—some reference pop culture, some reference science or history. The point is to engage a wide variety of people. At the end of the trivia, I give out prizes to the top participants.

For my nonfiction books, I like to stage a signing with a workshop. My audience for the Paper Hearts books are aspiring writers, so rather than just read from the books and do a traditional question-and-answer session, I present a workshop to my audience, complete with graphics on a projector and handouts the participants can take home.

Just because most people associate author events with readings doesn't mean you can't shift the dynamic into something creative, unique, and fun.

QUESTION & ANSWER

Most author events involve some form of Q&A. In fact, I've done whole events that were nothing but Q&A, and they are among my favorite events.

If you're worried no one will ask anything, pull aside some family and friends and give them some staged questions to ask in order to get the ball rolling. You can also offer a small prize to the first five or so people who ask a question—bite-sized candies work great for this, especially among teens.

When the questions start coming in—and they will—you can expect a few standbys that are always asked.

How much money do you make? A variation of this question is almost always asked. Remember that you don't have to answer a question you don't want to. You can either politely decline to answer, or give a glib answer. Just know that this question is likely coming, so think of how you want to answer it.

What's your inspiration? You'll hear this question so much you'll come to dread it. But remember that writing is an art form that not everyone understands, so try to be patient with this one. It's hard to explain the magic of writing—and harder still to explain how it's not magical at all, but a lot of work—but still, be respectful of your audience.

How do you get a book published? There is almost always an aspiring writer in your audience. Heck, a decade ago, *I* was that aspiring writer in your audience. Give an answer, but don't dwell too much on this one. How to get a book published is such a long answer that I have *literally written three books on the topic*, one of which you're currently holding in your hands. You simply cannot give a full answer here—and remember that the rest of your audience are readers, not writers, and they care about your book, not your job. Don't brush off the question, but also don't bore everyone in the audience who's not a writer just to satisfy the one person who is. If you can, give a condensed story of your publication journey and offer to talk to the author after the event. Feel free to recommend this book series as well. . .

Doing Group Events

GIVEN THE CHOICE, I much prefer doing group events over solo ones. They're so much more fun! And they're easier; you don't have to be "on" the whole time and can rely on your fellow participants to share the load.

When doing group events, it helps to select a theme for the event that you can then focus the program around. Find something in common with your book and the books of the other authors on the event. It can be your genre, but it could be something more specific than that—your heroines all kick ass, or there's a touch of magic in each novel, or each has a theme about overcoming huge odds. Find that common thread and exploit it so that the event is focused and centered.

This not only helps the event go more smoothly, but also helps in advertising the event. A "title" for the event makes it stand out on posters in the bookstore and gives the reader a better idea of what to expect.

Once you have a theme, select a moderator. This could be one of the authors, or it could be the bookstore employee or someone else involved. It doesn't have to be formal, but there should be someone whose job it is to keep the event moving along, to fill in empty silences with a new question, to help steer the dialogue, and to remind people to respect the time constraints.

This person should also be good at tactfully cutting off an author who's speaking too much. There's always someone on a panel who feels like they have to answer every question or whose stories get carried away and go long. I've been this person before, despite trying my best not to be—authors just love to tell stories! A good moderator can find a point to jump in to move the discussion to a new topic, or can focus a question to encourage the people who haven't had a chance to talk yet to speak up.

Most group events are panel discussions. Whenever you're on a panel, it's important for you to always appear engaged. When someone else is speaking, *listen*. Don't look bored, check your cellphone, or stare blankly ahead. First, it's disrespectful to the other people on the panel. Second, you'll look silly in pictures, and you can bet someone's taking pictures. And third, the audience will pick up on what you're doing. If you want your audience to listen to a speaker, *you* need to listen to the speaker.

Keep the format of a panel discussion as a discussion, not a checklist question-and-answer session. Don't just ask a question and everyone go down the line and answer it. That's boring and often repetitive. If your answer was already said, don't beat a dead horse; if you don't have anything to add, don't fill the silence with your voice just to speak. You don't have to answer every question. Instead, think of it like a dialogue. Jump in whenever you have something to contribute (although don't interrupt). If you know someone else has a better answer, let them answer. Set your fellow panelists up to give good answers.

At the end of the day, you want your audience to be entertained. If they like your style, they'll be interested in your book. They're already predisposed to like your work just by showing up to the event. So don't try to twist every answer into a thinly-veiled advertisement. Instead, engage in an interesting conversation that the reader will want to continue so much that she'll buy your book just to find out what else you have to say.

Online Video Events

SKYPE, SPREECAST, AND GOOGLE HANGOUTS tend to be the most commonly used forms of online video events. Skype is better suited for classroom visits; the other two are better suited for public events.

Before using any format, test it out with a friend and make sure that your equipment is good and that you are comfortable with the program. Never use a scheduled event as the first time you open up a program.

Beyond the basics, some things to keep in mind include:

Lighting: You need more than you think you do. If you need to set up a lamp shining directly in your face, do that. Err on the side of more lighting. Test out how you look with the windows open or not, with lights from the hallway on or not, or even consider setting up outside.

Color: The video quality of most of these programs is going to be a little poor. I have a specific tube of lipstick I call my "video lips"—it's a far brighter shade than I normally wear but works perfectly for video. I also try to avoid colors that will blend in with my background; if you have dark walls, wear white, and vice versa.

Sound: You may get better quality sound if you use headphones with a built-in mic; most people have a spare set of these lying around, so give them a try if you're having trouble with the sound.

Items: Keep anything you may want to talk about within easy reach. I always have copies of my books on a little side table beside me that I can grab if

I want to talk about that book. Ladies especially, try to avoid bending down and flashing your audience—keep things to your side rather than behind the camera or down low.

Book Festivals & Conventions

FESTS AND CONS ARE AMONG the most fun—and most work—you'll have as an author. They're a great place to meet fellow authors and a myriad of readers, and they're often filled with opportunities. Throw yourself into these events—but keep in mind these tips for surviving them.

KEEP YOUR KEY & YOUR SCHEDULE HANDY

Most fests and cons give you a name tag. They're usually those really big ones in a clear sleeve attached to a lanyard. *Use them.* Write up a small version of your schedule and put it behind your name tag so that all you have to do is glance at it and know when and where you're supposed to be next. And while you're at it, store your room key there—it's the perfect size, and this way you know you won't lose it. Especially important for us ladies who are cursed to have clothing without pockets.

If there's room, throw in a few singles behind your name badge so you can quickly and easily grab a coffee or soda between panels. And speaking of that—always carry some cash in small denominations when you travel to big group events. If you go out for a drink or quick lunch with other authors, it's so much easier to drop a ten on the table and leave if you have to rush off to another panel afterwards.

BOOK AT THE CON HOTEL & FIND THE GREEN ROOM

Whenever possible, book at the conference hotel. You will invariably get tired and want to take a break, even if just for ten minutes alone. Make it easy to escape to your room. If you can't book at the hotel, or if you can but it's a large con without easy access, see if there's a green room, conference room, or faculty lounge. Even if you don't think you'll use it, know where it is . . . you never know when you need a break from people.

HAVE A BOOK FOR DISPLAY

Most fests and cons won't provide you with a book to prop up on the table, but that doesn't mean you can't bring your own. Place it beside your name tag. It won't obscure your vision or your audience's sightline, but it will remind them of what you wrote.

If you can't display your book—perhaps there's no table, or it's too small—you can still hold it up when you introduce yourself.

LISTEN TO THE OTHER PANELISTS

I mentioned this in the previous chapter, but it bears repeating. Be attentive during your panels. Nothing looks more unprofessional that someone who only is interested in what's going on when they're speaking.

BRING WATER AND DRESS APPROPRIATELY

If you're like me, you don't talk much at home. I type; I don't speak! Which means when I *do* speak, I am quick to get a sore throat. Carry a water bottle with you to help offset that.

If your event is in a hotel, bring a light jacket. If it's outside, bring a small umbrella. Plan on worst case scenarios.

If you plan on wearing a dress or skirt, check to see if (a) you will be on a raised platform and (b) if the table will have a tablecloth that will hide your legs. An outfit that is perfectly discreet may not be that discreet when your knees are at eye-level with your audience. You may also want to consider the cut of your top if you're going to be sitting down and your audience will be standing and looking down at you and your cleavage.

KNOW WHERE SECURITY IS AND HOW TO REACH THEM

I hate that I have to include this, but not only have I heard too many horror stories, I've had some personal experience with con-goers who are inappropriate. Ask before the event where security will be located and who you should contact if you need security.

Keep in mind that some events include drinking—especially when the conference is taking place at a hotel. Beyond that, the larger the con, the greater the chance you'll run into a creeper.

If you feel threatened in any way, do *not* hesitate to get help *immediately*. Do not be polite to someone who threatens you or sexually harasses you. Do not worry about "losing a reader" and think that you need to just smile and nod. No. Do not put up with that shit. If you are threatened or harassed, get out of the situation as quickly as possible and seek help.

Organizing a Blog Tour

BLOG TOURS ARE WHERE BLOGS work together to post a series of articles or reviews about your book within a certain time frame. You can organize them yourself or with someone you hire, or sometimes your publisher will organize them.

LENGTH OF TOUR

Personally, I think a blog tour should only be about a week long. You'll want to share the tour across your own social media platforms, but you don't want to inundate your readers with links. A week has been a standard, good time frame that seems to have the most success for the majority of writers. You could have multiple posts up at different sites each day, although that's certainly not necessary.

TIMING OF TOUR

Aim for release week, give or take a week, if you're traditionally published. You're going to want strong sales straight out the gate, so your marketing push should be around that timeframe. Definitely don't do a blog tour if there's no way to purchase your book (no pre-order button or the book's not on sale)—that would be a waste of money. If you're self published, you may want to arrange a blog tour around a planned sale or to boost sales and reviews later on in publication, and it may arguably be better to wait to do a blog tour until you have some reviews in hand.

REQUESTING TOUR STOPS

If your publisher or a person you've hired is organizing the blog tour, then they should arrange the stops. Communicate early on if you have any stipulations or requirements. If, however, you're organizing the tour, you can approach the tour in two ways:

1. Solicit tour stops on your platform. If you have an extensive reach, you can create a sign up form and ask people to come to you. The advantage of this is using your existing fan base, which means you're likely to garner better reception and reviews. The disadvantage is that you may put yourself in a sticky situation—perhaps you get far too many sign-ups than you can reasonably handle and then have to drop some people from the tour. To avoid this, be clear from the start what you're looking for: a timeframe of when the tour is, how many stop you'd like, and a note saying that you can only provide content for so many bloggers and how you will select which ones you use.

2. Cold contact bloggers. This requires more leg work on your part, but can provide more quality blogs and attention to your book. To do this, make sure you follow the bloggers' guidelines. Approach each blogger individually, personally addressing them, explaining what you'd like to do. Err on the side of professional, even if you've been chatty with the blogger online in the past. The more information you can provide in the first email, the better. Don't send one line, "Would you like to do a blog tour with me?" Instead, spell out exactly what you want to do: "I'd like to do a five-stop tour. At each stop, I will be providing the blogger with an HTML-formatted guest article that's ready to post. I will also provide your readers with a giveaway of signed copies of my books." The more specific you are, the more likely they are to say yes.

TYPE OF TOUR

There are typically two types of tours: ones where the author provides the content, or ones where the bloggers provide reviews.

AUTHOR CONTENT FOR TOUR

The most common type of author-provided content for a blog tour tends to be interviews and guest posts. Be aware that this means the burden of work is on your shoulders, and if you have a fifty-stop tour, that is a *lot* of unique content to provide. If you're going to be doing this intense of a blog tour, take a step back and evaluate just how much work you can reasonably do within the timeframe without going crazy.

And also consider alternative types of content. Rather than focusing on quantity, focus on quality. This may mean limiting the number of stops on your tour, reducing them to a more reasonable workload. But it could also mean providing content that's not traditional interviews and guest posts. Perhaps organize a scavenger hunt, where readers need to go to every stop to piece together a clue or code. You could write a novella or short story for your novel, and provide each stop with a section of the novella or the whole short story. This is unique content that will drive readers to the blogs and your stories, and the only content you're creating is something that you can use in the future for marketing in other ways.

Remember: Err on the side of brevity. People are more likely to read a five-question interview than a fifty-question one. People are more likely to read a paragraph-long blog post than a page-long one. Lists work extremely well. Enhance your work with photographs and other media, and be focused on what the reader wants.

SAMPLE TOUR POST TOPICS

Create a list of twenty interview questions. Answer them all, then divide the question and answers among five to ten different bloggers, using the "mini-interviews" as the tour stops.

Create character profiles and have each stop feature a different character. Include photographs of actors in a dream movie casting, fun facts about the characters, a quote from each character, etc.

Divide your inspiration up into plot, world, and character. Create a post talking about the inspiration of the setting, and then several posts on the inspiration of the plot and characters (for example, talk about how one movie inspired this element and one work of art inspired this character and one book made you think of that character's name). Each post is a different tour stop.

If your book required a lot of research, divide the research into fun posts talking about the strange things you discovered. This doesn't have to be serious—you can talk about how you researched the fashion your characters wear or how you turned a vacation into a research trip.

When in doubt, make lists. They're short, they're easy to read, and they're the perfect content for blog tours. Examples:

- The top five sources of inspiration for my novel
- The three craziest things I learned when researching my novel
- Four hidden Easter eggs in my novel
- Three books that influenced my writing
- Eight things that surprised me about publishing my first novel
- Six things I wished I'd known before I wrote my book
- The three places I tend to write
- The five people I couldn't have written my book without
- The four things that happened to me in real life that ended up in my novel
- The three lines of my book that were hardest to write
- The four actors I used as models for my characters

REVIEW TOURS

Review tours are when bloggers get a book and agree to post a review of the book for the tour. I highly advise having someone other than the author organize this sort of tour—much like it's a bit gauche for you to throw yourself a party to ask for presents, it's better to have a publisher or a blog tour coordinator hired to organize such an event. There are several businesses that offer blog tour organization, and it's very simple to just pass the work off to them to organize and coordinate the efforts of the tour.

ORGANIZING THE CONTENT

If you're providing the content for a blog tour, the best thing you can do is make it as easy and professional as possible for the bloggers. If your publisher or a person you've hired is handling the blog tour, then it's their job to organize it all. If you're doing it on your own, though:

Remember that you're dealing with an online media. You know what doesn't really transcribe well to online platforms? Doc files from MS Word. If you write your blog post in Word, please, take it to an online platform and format it in html. It's very easy to use a free blogging platform, such as Blogger, to do this. Type your post up on the "Content" tab, adding in pictures and links, then just switch to the "HTML" tab and copy and paste what's there. The post will then be formatted for the blogger and ready to go. It's a little more work on your part, but gives the blogger a much easier job and makes your post look exactly the way you want it to look like.

FORMAT AND APPEARANCE OF CONTENT

Your blog tour is a specific promotional opportunity. Have a graphic that makes it easy for people to immediately see that the posts are a part of the tour. If you're providing the content yourself, you can format every page the same—graphic, introduction, buy-links to your book, placement of images and book cover, formatting of content. Consistent, professional appearance will make your tour stand out.

Organizing a Live Tour

DOING A SINGLE LIVE EVENT IS ONE THING, but what about doing a week of them?

Organizing a book tour can seem intimidating, but they're often both fun and rewarding. When you organize them yourself, without your publisher, you pay for them out of your own pocket—but they don't have to be very expensive, especially if you work with other authors.

The first tour I helped organize involved myself and two other authors. We went to eight cities, sold tons of books, had even more fun, met so many great people, and did it all for about $200 each.

When organizing a group book tour, it helps to know the other authors in advance. You're going to spend a lot of time with these people; make sure you get along. Discuss ahead of time the roles each person will play.

You can have a theme, but you don't have to. As long as the same audience would like all the books on tour, that's enough of a tie and enough of a reason to organize the events.

Before you go on tour, make sure you:

Communicate with your publisher. They are wise, experienced, have advice for you, and can help you come up with everything. Do this first.

Agree on finances. For my first group tour I helped organize, we decided to split everything equally three ways, with one person putting everything on her credit card and then dividing up the bill. We had a vague idea of a budget. But this should be the first thing you talk about.

Come up with places to tour. Are you driving or flying? Are the bookstores in the areas able to accommodate you? Develop a map of where you want to go and which bookstores you want to visit first, being reasonable with the time constraints of travel, and then contact the bookstores with the exact days and times you'd like to tour.

Decide on dates. Once you know where you want to go, consider when. Most authors do one event a day, but it's possible to double book if there are stores close enough together. However, you may think that a tour stop is simple and requires just a couple hours of time—but they are truly exhausting and take a lot out of you. So, in general, think about limiting how many times you double book, and don't forget to factor in travel and recuperation time!

Come up with an event agenda. Make sure that the bookstores know what to do. Send them a detailed agenda at least a week prior to the event if your program is more complicated (such as, "we would like someone at the store to moderate a panel and ask these questions"). Factor in at least an hour of programming and an hour of signing. Even if all you plan to do is show up and take questions, let the bookstore know.

Contact guests. If you're travelling to multiple cities, you may want to include a special local guest at some events. They can tag along to the tour stop closest to them. It's a nice way of including more people without adding much complication to the tour. Make sure to communicate with guest authors what their roles will be, and include them in marketing plans so they can help cross promote.

MARKETING: BEFORE & DURING

Marketing basically never ends from the moment you come up with the tour to the actual tour itself. Your biggest problem is to get people to actually *come* to the events.

Website: It's easy and free to set up a basic website to advertise a tour. Consider doing it on Tumblr, which allows easy sharing of posts. Make sure you have clear links to the authors on tour, details about the books, and a separate page for each tour stop so it's easy to link to and share.

Spread the News: In order to help spread the news, consider offering incentives for people to share. Have each author donate a signed copy of her book and provide a big prize of all the books for people who share information about the tour on social media. Make it easy for your readers with pre-made Facebook links, Twitter posts, and an easily downloadable widget for people to share.

Bookstore advertising: You can provide posters, bookmarks, and postcards to your bookstore prior to the event so they can distribute to their patrons.

Press releases: Write a short, one-page press release and send it to the local newspapers and magazines. Make sure to include contact information if the media would like to interview the authors on tour.

On-site giveaway: To encourage people to (a) come and (b) buy books, offer a giveaway just for people at the event, and gave them extra entries for every book they bought.

Social media: Use your already established social media contacts to remind people of the events and encourage them to come. Make sure to cross promote with all the authors on tour.

TOURING

Travel cheaply. If possible, carpool and find ways to minimize hotel costs, such as sharing a room or staying at friends' and family's homes.

Eat and sleep when you can. This is the best advice for anyone on tour ever.

Keep it light and entertaining. People attended book tours predominantly to (a) learn and (b) be entertained.

Money. Share costs equally. Between gas and travel expenses, paying for door prizes, printing materials, a tour may cost between $500 to $1,000, but when that is divided among 3-5 authors, the budget is much more doable.

Work Together. It's important for you to consider yourself, your fellow authors, and the bookstore owners as partners. Don't be a diva. Don't consider yourself better. Be willing to do work, and be willing to work with others. You'll get a lot more done that way.

Don't do all the work yourself: If you're working with others, share the load. One person can design posters, another writes the press release, and someone else can help with mailings.

Have Fun. This is not the time to try to one-up the people around you. Don't try to build yourself up by standing on the shoulders your fellow authors. One of the things we heard over and over when I did my first group tour was that people had fun because *we* were having fun. We heard horror stories from some of the bookstore owners about events where the person was just in it to sell books or prove something. It's a lot more fun to just . . . you know, have *fun.*

Be prepared for a lot of work. Most people only see the end result. They don't realize that, for a tour in August, the authors had been planning since February. They don't realize that the authors made the posters, websites, bookmarks, and everything else themselves—and that they paid for it all. But regardless of the work, know that going to bookstores and meeting readers is definitely worth it!

Surviving a Publisher Tour

SOMETIMES YOUR PUBLISHER WILL send you on a book tour. Congrats, that means you don't have to pay for costs, your publisher will take care of all the details, and you'll be zipped around the country, living the dream!

You're also going to end up exhausted, most likely sick, and incredibly stressed out. Here's some tips for making it through this experience.

PACK LIGHT

I'm a HUGE fan of keeping everything in a carry-on. You avoid the lines at baggage claim, and you avoid the risk of lost luggage. If you're in a group tour, you speed up the process and keep the packing of the car that picks you up light. If you can fit it into a carry on, do that.

Essentials to include:

• *Snacks.* High protein packs of nuts are great on tour for a quick pick-me-up, but anything that's easy and quick to stuff in your face between events is awesome. Anything with Vitamin C is also good.

• *Cash in small bills.* You may want to drop by a vending machine, pick up a coffee, or leave a tip. Keep some ones and fives in your wallet, easy to get to. (Note: if your publisher has arranged a car service for you, tip should be included—feel free to ask if you're worried about it. If you're saving receipts to get reimbursed later, tips probably aren't included—but keep track of them and add to your invoice.)

• *Band-Aids/first aid.* Something's going to go wrong, and you're going to have a bad day. Expect blisters, headaches, and stomachaches at the least. I have never been on a publisher tour where at least one person didn't get sick—and I've seen everything from food poisoning to stress-related allergies. If you take prescriptions, consider having a copy of the script on hand so you can get a refill if you leave your meds in a hotel.

• *Noise cancelling headphones/eye mask.* Think you can't sleep on a plane? Ha. Wait until the third day. Pro tip: wear ear plugs, then put your noise cancelling headphones on with just the noise cancelling sound going. You'll be able to sleep through surround-sound screaming-babies.

• *Phone charger.* If you have a spare, pack one in your luggage, only to be used if you lose the other. Pack the other one somewhere really easy to get to, so you can recharge at the airport or on the road.

• *Hand sanitizer.* You need so much hand sanitizer. Ohmygosh. Get some hand sanitizer. You know that one guy with a hacking cough on the airplane? Hello, seat mate. You know that kid who probably has the flu? That's the fan who travelled a hundred miles just to hug you. *Douse yourself with hand sanitizer.*

STAY HEALTHY

Sleep when you can, eat when you can. That is the true mantra of any author on tour.

DON'T BE AFRAID TO SAY NO

Authors tend to be introverts, which doesn't necessarily mean we're shy—it just means we re-charge by being in private instead of public. Unfortunately, book tour stops require pretty much the exact opposite of our natural lifestyle: The point is to go out and be in front of other people, and it's a very public experience.

Chances are, you're going to end up in a city where a friend or family member lives, and they're going to want to take you out for drinks or dinner. If you want to, do it. But if you're not up to it, just say no. You don't have to give an excuse to preserve your own sanity and health.

KEEP TRACK OF EXPENSES

Your publisher should be footing the bill for the transportation and hotel stays, and perhaps some arranged meals, but you'll likely encounter some unexpected expenses. Be sure to keep track of everything for reimbursement later—without a receipt, you probably won't get paid back.

Talk to your publisher first, but more than likely all hotel expenses, including in-room dining, will be included. It's often far easier to eat at the hotel than worrying about the receipts. Pro-tip: Don't be afraid to also order some wine with that meal. You earned it.

On Charging for Events

THERE ARE SOME THINGS NEARLY ALL authors do for "free." By "free," I mean that the author doesn't get a paycheck for showing up. But at the same time, they aren't truly free. Bookstore events are something for which an author doesn't get paid for her participation, but she indirectly profits from book sales at the event. Many conventions don't provide an honorarium to the author but do provide lodging, convention admission, and/or marketing opportunities.

Most events that authors consider charging a fee for are with schools and libraries—and that often creates a catch-22. Schools and libraries are beloved to authors; we *want* to present to them for free! But they also often require travel, a lot of time, and, frankly, work, and doing too many without charging a fee can negatively impact an author's career.

When I was a teacher, it was always a struggle to get authors to come do school visits in my small rural classroom.

I researched to find out which authors were within driving distance. I crafted lovely long emails, pleading with them about how my students were lower-income, how being in a rural area meant they rarely had the chance to see an author, about how much it would mean to them to have this experience.

And then I tried not to be disappointed when the authors responded with how much their fees were.

My school had no money for author visits. Well, not in the easy account. I could have written grants or begged with the principal to find some surplus, but work piled up and report cards were due and parent conferences were happening and . . . I just never went that route.

Instead, I groused to my fellow teachers that if I ever became a published author, *I* would never charge fees to schools.

One of the first events I did after *Across the Universe* came out was at the high school where I used to work. I was the hometown hero, and it was thrilling to present to the students I used to teach. There was a banquet for me in the library, complete with a custom cake, and students lined up down the hallway to get my signature.

This is why I do what I do, I thought smugly. All those authors out there who had fees attached to their presence were missing out—on this opportunity, on sales, on giving back.

I said yes to everything in driving distance for the first few years, and I interpreted driving distance as anything within two hundred miles or so. Some of the events were amazing—although none topped that first experience at my home school. The best class visits were where all the students had read the book ahead of time. One brilliant day was spent in a school on a Cherokee reservation; the teacher had bought both *Across the Universe* and *A Million Suns* for the class using a grant, and we had a pizza party and discussed stories.

But these great events stick out in my memory because there were so many events where the teacher used me as a substitute, some even leaving the campus entirely. Order forms disappeared, and even when I'd cart a case of books to the library, not a single student or teacher would buy one. I'd spend hours coming up with a program, complete with audio/visual, and students would sleep through it or no one would show up at the library. After school programs were entirely empty; no one had bothered to do more than announce my visit on the loudspeaker before class that day.

Of course, you can't judge all events based on the bad apples, but I'd be lying if I didn't say it wasn't disheartening. I started to dread doing events in general, and my usual optimism was quickly being replaced with jaded, low expectations.

I griped about one particular school event to another author, complaining that it had been sparsely attended, no one had bought a book, and the kids were entirely disinterested, several of them putting their heads down to sleep as soon as the teacher left the room.

"That's weird," he said. "I was just there and it was a great event. I sold a couple dozen copies and they filled the auditorium."

My eyes boggled. "What?" I asked. "Really?"

"Yeah," he said. "Let me guess; you did the event for free."

"Of course," I said. "How much did you charge?"

Turns out, he charged quite a bit. And the reception he got was miles different.

It came down to a sense of value. In his experience—and in mine, since then—whenever an event costs money, the perception is that it's *worth* money. When something's free, the perception is it's valueless. Even though, logically, we all know that's not how things work, we can't help but subconsciously rank the value of something free versus something not free. And even if that perception of value bias isn't there, event organizers have a stronger desire to make an event that's paid for succeed.

"Besides," the author said, "my attitude is: If I charge for the event, even if the event isn't that great, I've made up for my time in the fee."

It's worth noting that the author I was speaking to was male; nearly all my male writer friends charge a fee for events and don't feel guilty about it, while nearly all my female writer friends either charge a fee and feel guilty (usually waiving the fee if there's any pushback) or don't charge anything at all. I've often wondered if this contributes negatively to the gender bias in literary awards—a sort of trickle-down effect of the perceived value bias.

Regardless, as much as I wanted to give back to the schools and libraries that had helped me so much, I was starting to realize that my charity was benefitting no one—not me, not the students, not book sales or exposure. I personally didn't want to be perceived as less valuable, but more than that, I didn't want authors and books in general to be perceived as throwaways and time fillers. Additionally, *it's not wrong to be compensated for work.* There's giving back, and then there's doing work for free.

And make no mistake: Doing events is *work.* Yes, it's one of the best parts of my job, but it's still a part of my *job.* It takes away time—far more time than just the hour I'm speaking at the event. I have to make the program if it's not a question and answer session. I have to drive to and from the event. I have to smile and be chipper and happy and "on" for the entire event, from the moment I arrive to when I drive away. And honestly, I have to spend several hours before the event psyching myself up to be in public and several hours after detoxing from the experience. Ah, the joys of being an introvert. All this means that by the end of my one-hour event, I've lost easily one day of work, usually two or three.

This is not to say that I don't like doing events; it remains one of my favorite things. I enjoy talking with readers, I love to share my experience, and nothing replaces the thrill I have to know my words have meant something to someone else.

But being a career author means you have to balance writing with not-writing; things that make money with things that don't.

I started experimenting with fees. I still wanted to give back to the school and library systems, so I changed my policy to do free events at schools and libraries within driving distance if books were available for sale (through a local indie bookstore who does satellite events) and the program was simply a question and answer session. I started charging for any event that required more than an hour's travel and wanted a more complex program. I waived fees if books were purchased in advance—to me, book sales are equivalent to charging a fee—and I worked with out-of-area schools and libraries by doing a certain number of Skype sessions for free.

When I travel, I try to fit a (free) event to the places where I'm at. When I go to writing conferences, I reach out to schools and libraries in the area to see if they'd like me to drop in, if time allows. I've been known to fit events into my vacation plans—it really is something I love to do. I've just had to learn to balance my charity with my job, tempering the free events with paid ones.

PROS OF DOING EVENTS FOR FREE

- A sense of charity and giving back
- Benefitting organizations that promote reading
- Positive connections with libraries and schools
- Direct access and marketing to teen audiences
- Potential "snowball" effect; a reader may purchase the book later based on the presentation, greater chance for word-of-mouth sales to grow

CONS OF DOING EVENTS FOR FREE

- Devaluation of work (both of the presentation and your novel)
- Lack of direct sales (if the organization doesn't provide or allow them)
- Time to create presentation
- Travel expenses
- Greater likelihood of poor reception and low audience attendance and participation
- Bucks the idea that "work deserves payment" for other authors who do charge a fee; sets a negative precedent for fair wages

Getting Paid for Events

WHETHER YOU'RE ESTABLISHING your fees for events or whether an organization approaches you to do an event and asks your rates, you need to be prepared to talk about money.

Consider how much your time is worth. In any creative career, time is money, and I often lose a whole day of work for a simple thirty minutes of discussing writing with students via Skype. When I can't write due to events, I have to balance that time spent with monetary compensation.

HOW MUCH TO CHARGE

Establish rates early, and have them in a place where people can easily review them. I tend to vary rates depending on how far I have to travel and the format of the program—if it's a group event or an event where books are sold, it's easier for me to participate and therefore I charge less. If it's a program where I have to speak on my own and essentially actively teach a lesson, that's more work and more difficult for me to do, so I charge more.

In the end, how much you personally charge often depends on your own comfort level. An honorarium of $100 per hour is a low but respectable rate for an established author, but prices certainly vary depending on the author's comfort zone in speaking publicly. I know several authors who still do events for free; I know some who charge more than $2000 a day. An average would probably be around $250 per hour; $500 for a half-day; $1,000 for a whole day. A single key-note speech would charge between $100-$500.

Evaluate how much your time and energy is worth to you. You don't have to make excuses for charging fees for events; simply present what the fees are.

HOW TO APPROACH FEES

Many times an organization will inquire about an event without bringing up fees. A good way to respond without letting the awkward conversation dance around the subject of money is to be direct. For example:

> *Thanks for asking me to come speak to your classroom! Because you're outside my local area, which requires me to add on travel costs, my fee for a half-day event at your school is $500. If this isn't within your means, please let me know and I can work with you and your budget.*

I always try to give the inquirer a way to work with me without paying the full price; I know many schools can't afford fees. By offering to work with them, you may be able to find a compromise that benefits you both, such as changing a live event that requires travel time to a Skype visit that requires far less time and effort on my part.

CHARGING FOR ONLINE EVENTS

Just because an event isn't live doesn't mean it should be free—it still takes time and effort. If you want to charge for a Skype visit or similar, absolutely feel free to do so. Rates tend to be lower for an online event than a live one, so base your prices accordingly. And make sure you're clear upfront that online events require fees, and why.

PRO BONO

Consider doing a portion of events for free. Right now, my policy is to give two free Skype visits to a school or library a year. Once I reach my free limit, I still offer to do Skype visits, but only for my fee. This also helps me when I have to eventually say that I have to charge—I can explain that I do some events free, but have reached my quota. Some people tend to get angry when an author charges a fee, but when I explain that I have done some events for free, it helps them understand that I simply can't do *all* of them without earning a paycheck for my work. It also gives them the opportunity to wait until the following year to request a free Skype event.

Another compromise of doing events for free is to offer to do them if the host can either guarantee a certain number of sales or offer sales at the event. Some authors offer a free event to any classroom library that has bought X number of books—a great opportunity for book clubs. Others are fine doing a free event, especially a live one, as long as it's possible to offer sales before or after the event on location. These sorts of events may pay for themselves in sales.

Even if you're doing the event for free, consider sending the school an invoice—not to charge them, but to show them what you typically charge, and the bill zeroed out. You can also check with your accountant to see if pro bono events will count as charity when it comes to tax write-offs.

WAYS TO LOWER COSTS

If you really want to do events but cannot afford to do them without pay, there are some creative ways to lower the costs to the host event.

If you're going to be in a certain area for a convention or book signing anyway, reach out to local schools and libraries and see if they're interested in hosting you for a free or reduced rate, since you'll be in the area anyway. You can also talk to the bookstores in the area; many of them have connections with local schools and libraries and can facilitate more sales on location for you.

Ask schools and libraries to pool resources. If you have to travel and the school only wants you for one session, reach out to a neighboring school and see if they can hire you for a second one so you can offset the travel costs.

You may also want to look up some local grants that you can suggest that schools apply to, or provide links to grants so you can point organizers to them.

DON'T FORGET TRAVEL EXPENSES

Regardless of how much you charge for your speaking fee, keep in mind that travel expenses add up. Not only do you have to pay for gas and possibly even flights and hotels, but travel adds to the time away from writing. An hour long trip may just be an additional $20 in gas, but it's also an hour of lost work time.

Always confirm what expenses are covered when negotiating fees for events outside your local area—and do it early. Don't agree to an out-of-state event assuming you'll get paid without confirming this first.

The Introvert's Guide to Selling Books

TO A LOT OF PEOPLE, I SEEM LIKE an extrovert. I'm not that shy, and I'm okay in front of audiences. But I'm actually very introverted. My friend and fellow author Andrea Cremer summed it up perfectly: an extrovert gets energy from being around other people; an introvert recharges by being alone. And in those terms, I'm extraordinarily introverted. I *can* be in a crowd or in front of audiences, but it *drains* me. Being social is as draining for me as working out. Even being on Skype—this is why I limit the number of events and I do. Doing an event for an hour takes me all day to hype myself up and then to recover after. In very stressful, very big events, I will often just sit in silence in a room by myself to recover.

So conventions and book fests, packed to the brim with people, is like an Iron Man Triathlon to me.

Be organized. Get your schedule and study it. Figure out where you have "on" time and where you have down time, and make sure you have the down time you need. And when you can't get down time, come up with a plan. Don't have time to go back to your hotel room? Go to the green room, ask for a quiet room, or even just locate the nearest bathroom and catch five minutes alone.

Get help. If you can, have someone with you, such as a spouse or friend, at big events. Put them to work handing out the promo stuff while you start your panels, carting books around, taking care of the money during sales. That last one is key; whenever possible, always let someone other than the author be in charge of money.

Use social media at live events. It's so simple, but so easy to forget—just because you're at a live event doesn't mean your online audience isn't participating.

A few weeks before the event: The schedule may not be final yet, but let people know where you'll be and whether or not you'll be signing and/or selling books.

The week of the event: Post your schedule everywhere, and make sure it's visible throughout the event. Fans who've come to see you at the con will have an easier time of it if you show when and where you're accessible.

Fifteen minutes before a panel or signing: Tweet or otherwise use social media, and use the event's hashtag. This helps people who are the event see you—imagine a convention attendee stuck between panels, scrolling through Twitter, and seeing your signing.

Remember: don't harass your social media followers, especially the ones not there. Tell the people about your stuff, but don't go overboard.

At signings, make your stuff do the talking so you don't have to. Before panels, ask your helper to pass out cards or swag with your book's information. Have a copy of your book on the table during your panel.

At signings, some people are really in favor of what I call the "car salesman approach." They stand up at their table, they literally pull people over and pitch their books. They're charismatic and they draw people in and they sell their books with everything they have. It works. But it doesn't work for *me*. I can't do that. I can't be that person.

But it's also not effective to just sit there. So design your table so passers-by can see what you write without you having to do a hard sell. At many book festivals or conventions, your table will look like this:

Just a table, a water pitcher, and two chairs. And most authors will leave it like that.

But you can add more:

Sign in the front of the table. People are curious about what you're doing at the table, but they also know that if they approach to find out, they might be pulled into a hard sales pitch they're not interested in. So I made the sign to tell them who I am and what I have to offer, so they can walk on by if they're not interested . . . or stop if they are. It is a braggy sign—I have the *NY Times* list information, a Kirkus Star, and a pull quote. And it labels me as author; sometimes people don't always realize the person sitting behind the books is actually the author. I made it colorful and chatty, and the poster is laminated and reusable.

Book display set up. It's hard to see in this picture, but I actually have stacks of books behind each of the Across the Universe books, and anyone walking by could see I had stock. My husband sat in the chair beside me, behind the books, with a bag of change and a card reader, so there was no doubt that books were on sale. Having the stock there and readily available (and visible) signaled to people that it was available.

Freebies that I was very free with. I had post cards, pin buttons, and more sitting on the table, and one of the first things I said to anyone who approached was to take something for free. People are interested in free. It gives them something to talk about, something to have in their hands, and it takes the pressure off me to be the salesman. The husband handled the money and sold the books—I gave out the free stuff.

Sign up forms. I used two: one for pre-orders of my new book, and one for sign ups to my newsletter. Even if people didn't want to buy things, they could stay up to date on future things, and several people took this opportunity.

Listen. I put the table on the offensive—it did my introductions for me. Which let me be in the position where I could bypass my introduction and listen to my readers as they approached. It gave them the chance to set the stage for our conversation. It gave them the opportunity to talk first, which let me listen. Introverts are much better at listening than talking, and as a writer, I would much rather listen to my readers than talk at them.

Think of your table at a big signing in a convention or book festival as a battle station. Be prepared to go to war . . . or at least sign some books.

In the End...

The Most Important Thing

REMEMBER: NOTHING MARKETS A BOOK better than the next book. And you're doing this for the books—not the money, not the fame, not the whatever.

So go write your next book.

About the Author

Beth Revis is the author of the *New York Times* bestselling novel *Across the Universe* and its sequels, as well as *The Body Electric,* more than a dozen published short stories, and a forthcoming YA novel from Penguin/Razorbill. She currently lives in rural North Carolina with her boys: one husband, one son, and two massive dogs.

Prior to becoming a full time novelist, Beth spent a lot of time writing books that didn't sell. *Paper Hearts* is the book series she wished she had during that time.

Would you like Beth to speak to your writer's group? Please contact her at authorbethrevis@gmail.com for rates and availability.

Find Beth online at bethrevis.com. Sign up for her newsletter at http://bit.ly/bethnews and never miss a new release.

 @bethrevis

@authorbethrevis

Praise for Beth's Novels

ACROSS THE UNIVERSE

"Who Should Read This: Well, sci-fi and mystery fans will love it, but so will any girl or boy who's ever sat in a room full of quiet conformists and wanted to scream at them all, 'Wake up!'" —MTV.com

A MILLION SUNS

"Setting and plot are the heart and soul of this ripping space thriller, and they're unforgettable." —*Kirkus*, starred review

SHADES OF EARTH

"[Revis has a gift] as a propulsive storyteller with a knack for jarring surprises and raising the stakes." —*Booklist*

THE BODY ELECTRIC

"Short chapters…make for addictive reading, and the reverie-within-reverie sequences are vibrantly rendered games of cat and mouse. …Revis gives a masterly blend of worlds familiar and new in this standalone SF mystery." —*Publisher's Weekly*

A WORLD WITHOUT YOU

A stunning tale of heroes and death, adventure and mental illness, coming in summer 2016 from Penguin/Razorbill!

Thank You for Reading

Please consider leaving a review for this and the other Paper Hearts books on your favorite retailer or review site. Reviews help new readers find these and other great books.

CPSIA information can be obtained
at www.ICGtesting.com
Printed in the USA
FFOW03n0957190716
26019FF

9 780990 662693